# TRACING YOUR SCOTTISH FAMILY HISTORY ON THE INTERNET

# FAMILY HISTORY FROM PEN & SWORD BOOKS

*Birth, Marriage & Death Records*
*The Family History Web Directory*
*Tracing British Battalions on the Somme*
*Tracing Great War Ancestors*
*Tracing History Through Title Deeds*
*Tracing Secret Service Ancestors*
*Tracing the Rifle Volunteers*
*Tracing Your Air Force Ancestors*
*Tracing Your Ancestors*
*Tracing Your Ancestors from 1066 to 1837*
*Tracing Your Ancestors Through Death Records –*
*Second Edition*
*Tracing Your Ancestors through Family*
*Photographs*
*Tracing Your Ancestors Through Letters and*
*Personal Writings*
*Tracing Your Ancestors Using DNA*
*Tracing Your Ancestors Using the Census*
*Tracing Your Ancestors: Cambridgeshire, Essex,*
*Norfolk and Suffolk*
*Tracing Your Aristocratic Ancestors*
*Tracing Your Army Ancestors*
*Tracing Your Army Ancestors – Third Edition*
*Tracing Your Birmingham Ancestors*
*Tracing Your Black Country Ancestors*
*Tracing Your Boer War Ancestors*
*Tracing Your British Indian Ancestors*
*Tracing Your Canal Ancestors*
*Tracing Your Channel Islands Ancestors*
*Tracing Your Church of England Ancestors*
*Tracing Your Criminal Ancestors*
*Tracing Your Docker Ancestors*
*Tracing Your East Anglian Ancestors*
*Tracing Your East End Ancestors*
*Tracing Your Family History on the Internet*
*Tracing Your Female Ancestors*
*Tracing Your First World War Ancestors*
*Tracing Your Freemason, Friendly Society and*
*Trade Union Ancestors*
*Tracing Your Georgian Ancestors, 1714–1837*
*Tracing Your Glasgow Ancestors*
*Tracing Your Great War Ancestors: The Gallipoli*
*Campaign*
*Tracing Your Great War Ancestors: The Somme*

*Tracing Your Great War Ancestors: Ypres*
*Tracing Your Huguenot Ancestors*
*Tracing Your Insolvent Ancestors*
*Tracing Your Irish Family History on the Internet*
*Tracing Your Jewish Ancestors*
*Tracing Your Jewish Ancestors – Second Edition*
*Tracing Your Labour Movement Ancestors*
*Tracing Your Legal Ancestors*
*Tracing Your Liverpool Ancestors*
*Tracing Your Liverpool Ancestors – Second*
*Edition*
*Tracing Your London Ancestors*
*Tracing Your Medical Ancestors*
*Tracing Your Merchant Navy Ancestors*
*Tracing Your Northern Ancestors*
*Tracing Your Northern Irish Ancestors*
*Tracing Your Northern Irish Ancestors – Second*
*Edition*
*Tracing Your Oxfordshire Ancestors*
*Tracing Your Pauper Ancestors*
*Tracing Your Police Ancestors*
*Tracing Your Potteries Ancestors*
*Tracing Your Pre-Victorian Ancestors*
*Tracing Your Prisoner of War Ancestors: The First*
*World War*
*Tracing Your Railway Ancestors*
*Tracing Your Roman Catholic Ancestors*
*Tracing Your Royal Marine Ancestors*
*Tracing Your Rural Ancestors*
*Tracing Your Scottish Ancestry Through Church*
*and State Records*
*Tracing Your Scottish Ancestors*
*Tracing Your Second World War Ancestors*
*Tracing Your Servant Ancestors*
*Tracing Your Service Women Ancestors*
*Tracing Your Shipbuilding Ancestors*
*Tracing Your Tank Ancestors*
*Tracing Your Textile Ancestors*
*Tracing Your Twentieth-Century Ancestors*
*Tracing Your Welsh Ancestors*
*Tracing Your West Country Ancestors*
*Tracing Your Yorkshire Ancestors*
*Writing Your Family History*
*Your Irish Ancestors*

# TRACING YOUR SCOTTISH FAMILY HISTORY ON THE INTERNET

*A Guide for Family Historians*

## CHRIS PATON

Pen & Sword
**FAMILY HISTORY**

First published in Great Britain in 2020 and reprinted in 2020 by
**PEN AND SWORD FAMILY HISTORY**
An imprint of
Pen & Sword Books Ltd
Yorkshire – Philadelphia

ISBN 978 1 52676 838 4

Printed in the UK by CPI Group (UK) Ltd, Croydon, CR0 4YY

Pen & Sword Books Limited incorporates the imprints of Atlas,
Archaeology, Aviation, Discovery, Family History, Fiction, History,
Maritime, Military, Military Classics, Politics, Select, Transport,  True
Crime, Air World, Frontline Publishing, Leo Cooper, Remember
When, Seaforth Publishing, The Praetorian Press, Wharncliffe  Local
History, Wharncliffe Transport, Wharncliffe True Crime
and White Owl.

For a complete list of Pen & Sword titles please contact

PEN & SWORD BOOKS LIMITED
47 Church Street, Barnsley, South Yorkshire, S70 2AS, England
E-mail: enquiries@pen-and-sword.co.uk
Website: www.pen-and-sword.co.uk

Or

PEN AND SWORD BOOKS
1950 Lawrence Rd, Havertown, PA 19083, USA
E-mail: Uspen-and-sword@casematepublishers.com
Website: www.penandswordbooks.com

# CONTENTS

# INTRODUCTION

Although I was born in Northern Ireland, I spent the first four years of my life living in Scotland, with my father working as a submariner at the Faslane naval base near Helensburgh. After years of subsequent residence both within England and Northern Ireland, I returned to Scotland in 1997, and have lived here ever since.

As a small child I was always aware of a Scottish connection within my family. My grandmother Jean Paton, née Currie, was born in Glasgow, but despite moving to Northern Ireland in the late 1930s, she never lost her native Bridgeton brogue. As is often the way with family history, I had assumed that the Scottish side of my ancestral research would be concerned with my Scottish granny and her family, but I soon discovered that Jean's parents were actually Protestant Irish immigrants from County Londonderry in the late nineteenth century. It transpired that my connections to Scotland were in fact much more deeply rooted through the Paton side of my family, with my surname line hailing from Perthshire, and with various other family lines from Perthshire, Invernessshire and Lanarkshire.

When I first started to look into my ancestry, I was based in Glasgow and worked full-time in television production, meaning that the only way that I could

*Charles Paton, the author's grandfather, in Belgium, 1907. Although Charles was born in Brussels in 1904, his parents were both Scottish.*

carry out research was to use online resources in my evenings off and at weekends. Fortunately for me, my interest coincided with the start of a digital revolution, meaning that I could make a substantial amount of progress from home. When the history of the Scottish family history industry is written someday, it will inevitably focus to some degree on the Scottish Government's ScotlandsPeople website, but it was in fact its predecessor, Scots Origins, which first paved the way, providing the initial access to censuses and indexes for records held at the General Register Office for Scotland.

Things have moved on dramatically since then, and in this book I will explore the wealth of online resources available today to assist with Scottish family history research. For those living beyond Scotland it is important to note that while Scotland has been a part of the United Kingdom since 1801, and a part of Great Britain since 1707, its legal system, state church and education provision remained completely independent upon the formation of its union with England and Wales. In most areas things are similar – but different!

Should you require further background reading on many of the state-generated records referred to in this book, I would suggest consulting my previous book, *Tracing Your Scottish Ancestry Through Church and State Records*, also published by Pen & Sword. If your Scottish ancestors moved from beyond Scotland to settle elsewhere in England, Wales, Northern Ireland or the Republic of Ireland, my further guides, *Tracing Your Family History on the Internet* (2nd edition) and *Tracing Your Irish Family History on the Internet* (2nd edition) may be of some further assistance.

Websites do occasionally pass on and make their way to a digital heaven. In some cases, it is possible to visit 'dead' websites if the pages have been 'cached' (snapshot) by an internet library, such as the Internet Archive's 'Wayback Machine' at **https://archive.org/web/web.php**. Indeed, in this guide I have used this site to retrieve some resources which ventured forth to the great beyond some years ago, but which remain as useful now in their digital afterlife as when hosted on their original platforms. In a small number of cases I have also truncated long website addresses to an easier-to-type version using the Bit.ly website at **https://bitly.com**.

A huge thank you must go to Rupert Harding, Simon Fowler, Amy Jordan and the team at Pen & Sword for producing this book, to my wife Claire, and sons Calum and Jamie, for their ongoing support, and to all who help to make Scotland's unique history and heritage a little more accessible online by the day.

Finally, I'd like to pass on the greatest bit of Scottish genealogical wisdom that I have ever read, as conveyed by my Perth-based five-times-great-uncle Dr William Henderson, in his 1870 book *Bygone Days; or, Sketches Illustrative of the Manners and Customs of the Scottish Peasantry Seventy Years Ago (by an Octogenerian)*:

> In my estimation, a long line of ancestry entitles no man to trample on his brother, nor does a high sounding title give its possessor a right to wound the heart, which vibrates with the finer feelings of a common humanity, merely because accident has cast his lot in an elevated station of life, which he degrades by his vices, and in doing so prostrates the gifts of Providence, and makes them the means of wounding the peace and ruining the prospects of thousands, who though below him in station are nevertheless immeasurably raised above him in talent, in virtue, and proper feeling. Whether in prince or in peasant a genuine heart elicits from me the response of a brother.

It's about as Scottish a line of advice as you will ever read, and essentially advises us that we are all Jock Tamson's bairns!

# Chapter 1

# GATEWAYS AND INSTITUTIONS

The information that we must gather for genealogical research comes in the form of both primary and secondary sources, and such material, as found online, is no different. Primary sources are original documents, recordings or testimonies, while secondary sources are those which provide a story 'second hand' or which create a 'finding aid' to the original. It is always preferable to find a primary source, if it has survived, to see for yourself the most immediate record of any event.

The quality of information found is every bit as important as the quantity, and it is essential to bear in mind that in every case this is only as good as what has been presented to the writer who documented the relevant proceedings. Records can mislead – a wrong age given by the vain, an incorrect marital status by the serial bigamist, a false claim to the aristocracy in the name of social advancement. It is therefore important to check and double-check any records found wherever possible against other sources.

Sometimes when we experience problems, the fault is not with the record or the website, but with our expectations. Surnames have not always been spelt the same way, for example, and often what we are looking for is what someone else assumed a name was when it was recorded, and not what the holder of that name believed it to be. In one example of an Irish gent called Eoin Brogan who settled in Scotland, I invariably found him in different vital records documents listed as Owen Brogan, Iain Brogan, Yohan Brogan and John Brogan, clearly challenging every registrar he encountered. We may need to be more lateral in our approach, by using name variants, wildcards and other search techniques, or by being better educated about the environments within which our ancestors lived.

It is also worth considering that finding an individual with the right name in the right place at the right time does not necessarily mean that you have found the right person! The pool of personal names in times past was considerably more limited, and you may not be looking at a complete record set. Unique Scottish conventions such as the use of 'tee names' (nicknames) in the north-east of the country can also help to confuse matters further, as well as 'pet forms' of names, such as Jessie for Janet, and Peter instead of Patrick. Good luck also when trying to find out about your Great Auntie Ina – 'Ina' is a contraction of many women's names ending in '-ina', such as Donaldina, Wilhelmina, Charlesina, Thomasina. It was essentially a means to create a feminine form of a male forename.

Understanding the nature of the records found on a website, and the scope of the material included, is extremely important. Above all, despite its great strengths and advantages, never forget that not everything is online, and what is not yet available on the internet can be equally as important as what is. On any website, it never hurts to first spend some time looking at the help section and any relevant guides before seeking to plunder the relevant databases. Remember that the internet is also simply a library of resources – a massive repository of possibilities – but that there are many other resources available offline, to be neglected at your peril!

### Recording information

No matter which websites you consult, keep a note of their addresses and what information you have gleaned from them. You can store website addresses (URLs) on your browser's 'Favourites' tool, saving you having to retype the addresses on future visits. Be aware that some may change from time to time, particularly those from local authorities, and that information remains online in most cases only so long as the host platform is still around, or while the person who created the resource is still maintaining it.

It is always advisable to make a copy of any information discovered as soon as you find it. You can type out relevant portions, cut and paste text, save the web page as a file to be consulted offline, print off the page, or take 'screen grabs' (using your 'Print Screen' button). If a site does go down for any reason, all may not be lost – platforms such as the Internet Archive's Wayback Machine (**https://archive.org**) or the British Library's Web Archive (**www.webarchive.org.uk**) actually save many sites for posterity at regular intervals, allowing you to see earlier versions of the required page before its eventual demise.

You can choose to save your family tree and your research notes online through various resources, including online tree providers (p. 24).

Be wary of what you place online, however, most notably when it comes to the issue of privacy for people who are alive. As a rough rule of thumb, do not place details of people online who are still alive and/or born less than a century ago, and you should be covered. There may also be copyright implications for any documents you wish to place online, including old family photographs.

The law offers many protections to individuals who feel that their privacy has been violated, not least through the provisions of the EU's General Data Protection Regulation (GDPR), which was adopted into law in the UK from May 2018. Professional genealogists and organisations offering genealogical services should register with the Information Commissioner's Office (**https://ico.org.uk**) as a data processor. The ICO's guide on data protection and the GDPR is particularly useful at **https://ico.org.uk/for-organisations/guide-to-data-protection**.

## Gateway sites

There are many sites offering research guides for Scottish family history topics, including ScotlandsPeople (see Chapter 1) the National Records of Scotland (p.4) and the Scottish Archive Network (p.8). Additional 'gateway' platforms also exist, providing information and links to further resources.

The Scotland section of the GENUKI platform (**www.genuki.org.uk**) offers a range of topic selections from 'Almanacs' to 'Yearbooks'. Its interactive map allows you to visit dedicated pages for each of Scotland's historic counties, each county being identified with a three-letter 'Chapman

*The GENUKI Scottish page offers a gateway to many online resources.*

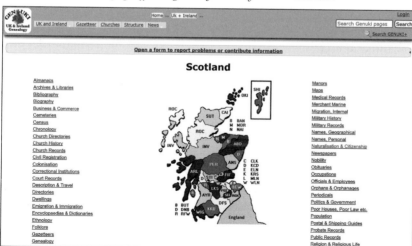

code', such as 'LKS' for Lanarkshire (a full list of Chapman codes is available at **www.genuki.org.uk/big/Regions/Codes**). Clicking through on an individual county brings you to a dedicated page for that area, with a map showing its position within Scotland, and a range of new topic headings, commencing with 'Archives & Libraries' and offering an introduction to each region. Under the county map is another link marked 'Town and Parishes', providing access to additional and more localised information and resources. GENUKI is a volunteer-based project, with some pages more detailed than others.

Scotland's Family (**www.scotlandsfamily.com**) is worth visiting for resources, such as parish maps and records indexes, although some links are broken. Another incredibly useful site is Cyndi's List, and its Scotland portal at **www.cyndislist.com/uk/sct/** offers a further range of topic headings for resources found online, from 'Birth, Marriage, Death' to 'Wills & Probate'. Additional resources may also be listed under the site's 'United Kingdom & Ireland' category at **www.cyndislist.com/uk**, and through other thematic topic headings.

The 'UK' family of sites from Ian and Sharon Hartas is a series of free-to-access directories providing links to resources from both a county or subject-based search, with Scotland well catered for. The sites include UK Births, Marriages, Deaths and Censuses on the Internet (**www. ukbmd.org.uk**), UK Genealogical Directories and Lists on the Internet (**www.ukgdl.org.uk**), and UK Military Family History on the Internet (**www.ukmfh.org.uk**). There is a degree of overlap to the links reported between the sites, but all should be consulted.

## The National Records of Scotland (NRS)
**www.nrscotland.gov.uk**
The National Records of Scotland was formed in April 2011 by a merger of the National Archives of Scotland and the General Register Office for Scotland. As an agency it offers two main research facilities, the ScotlandsPeople Centre, providing access to the ScotlandsPeople database (see Chapter 1), and the Historical Search Room for further archive-based research.

The NRS website is one of the most important websites to bookmark for Scottish research. While the home page offers news updates and various details about the legal services and roles fulfilled by the agency, and some useful genealogical links to resources such as the 1939 National Identity Register, the key area of the site for family historians is that for 'Research', which provides eight important categories of interest:

## i) Catalogues and Indexes

There are three main search tools offered via the NRS website. The institution's own catalogue (**https://catalogue.nrscotland.gov.uk/nrs onlinecatalogue/welcome.aspx**) allows you to search for an item in the archive by a word, several words or an exact phrase, a reference number and a date range (with a tick box to include results for records which are undated). An important consideration when performing a search is to note the access status alongside any results. Not all records are stored on site, and some may need to be pre-ordered prior to a visit; others may not be fit for production, for example, if requiring conservation work. Many records have also been digitised and made available on site through a computer system called Virtual Volumes, which is not accessible online.

The National Register of Archives for Scotland (**https://catalogue. nrscotland.gov.uk/nrasregister/welcome.aspx**) was founded in 1946 with a mission to catalogue private records holdings, including materials for private landed estates and individuals, businesses, museums, legal firms and other agencies. Much of what has been surveyed can be consulted via the NRAS Online Catalogue, but in a restricted format for some of the collections (and not at all for others); note that the full catalogue can only be consulted at the NRS, the National Library of Scotland (p.9) or the National Archives in England (p.8).

If a private collection has been catalogued you can write to the owner or holder via the NRAS and request access, but take note of the last line of advice given by the body on its webpage: 'access to private papers is a privilege and not a right'. Note that there is also a National Register of Archives at the National Archives (TNA) in England, the contents of which are now searchable through its Discovery catalogue (p.9). This lists some 44,000 unpublished lists and catalogues detailing the locations of additionally held private materials across the UK.

Lastly, the Scottish Archive Network catalogue (p.8) for local archive holdings can also be accessed via the NRS website.

## ii) Research Guides

The NRS has a wealth of material in its possession, and great expertise in explaining what it contains. The site's 'Research Guides A-Z' carries detailed descriptions of record types, from 'Adoption Records' to 'Wills and Testaments', which must absolutely be consulted before any visit. Each page will provide a history of the types of records and institutions of interest, as well as search tips, advice, and importantly, details of what it does hold, and what it does not.

In some examples, the site will have many sub-pages offering additional details. The page on 'Censuses', for example, has additional guides on each individual census from 1841–1911, another on pre-1841 censuses, a page with details on Webster's Account of the Population of Scotland in 1755 (including a link to an online hosted version), and various useful Further Reading suggestions.

### iii) Visit Us
This page offers various details about the different facilities available for research at the institutions, including its Research Library and Search Room User Group minutes, as well as opening hours, status updates, and visitor facilities.

### iv) Researching Online
This section provides a basic overview of online services, including ScotlandsPeople (see Chapter 1) and ScotlandsPlaces (p.14).

There is also a link to the NRS Web Continuity Service, which regularly caches pages from various bodies and makes them accessible through its NRS Web Archive. This includes material from the Scottish Government, the Scottish Parliament, Scottish public authorities, Scottish Courts, Scottish Public Inquiries, and private organisations which deposit archival records with the NRS.

### v) Learning
The NRS works with schools and other bodies to try to promote the use and understanding of archives. This section of its website provides links to resources for schools and on featured topics, publications, and resources for understanding palaeography, including a link to the Scottish Handwriting website (p.28).

### vi) Family History
On this page the NRS provides an overview of the key records useful for ancestral research in Scotland, complementing its similar guides on the ScotlandsPeople website (Chapter 1).

### vii) Events, Talks and Visits
The NRS regularly holds a talks programme at its New Register House building, which are free to attend, but for which you need to book.

Some of the NRS talks are recorded and repackaged as podcasts, which are later made available through the organisation's Open Book blog at **https://blog.nrscotland.gov.uk**.

*The National Records of Scotland website hosts the archive's catalogue and many important research guides.*

### *viii)* Hall of Fame A-Z

This section of the site provides short biographical summaries of the great and the good in Scotland, focussing on NRS records, which can help to shed a light on their documented existence.

If you are interested in the work of the NRS, another page well worth exploring is the 'Record Keeping' section at **www.nrscotland.gov.uk/ record-keeping**, where you can learn about the archive's statutory role, and its efforts in the preservation and conservation of historic documents.

### Local archives

In addition to the NRS there is a range of further archives across the country, including those of local authorities, universities, museums and in private collections. One thing to be wary of when it comes to local authorities is that they seem to change their websites with frustrating regularity. Should any link for a favoured site fall dead, return to the relevant council's home page and search for its archives and/or local studies pages from there.

The Scottish Council on Archives (**www.scottisharchives.org.uk**) is a body which advocates on behalf of the Scottish archive sector. The 'Explore' section of its website offers many valuable tools, including its 'Scottish Archives Map' page. This not only has an interactive map showcasing the locations of archives across Scotland, but it also provides a 'Browse Archives by Area' facility to the bottom of the page, with access to contact details, collections descriptions and more by region.

The National Archives in London also hosts a 'Find an archive in the UK and beyond' page (p.9), with a dedicated section for Scotland offering links to websites for archives, museums and libraries across the country. For those working in the archive sector, the Scotland page of the Archives and Records Association UK and Ireland website may be of interest at **www.archives.org.uk/about/nations-and-regions/ara-scotland.html**.

Another immensely handy resource is the Scottish Archive Network (SCAN) at **www.scan.org.uk**. SCAN was established in the 1990s as a collaborative project between the NRS, the Heritage Lottery Fund, and the Genealogical Society of Utah (the parent body behind FamilySearch), its aim being to digitise records and to catalogue archive holdings from across the country. On the digitisation front, its most successful effort was with Scottish wills and testaments, initially hosted on the Scottish Documents site (**www.scottishdocuments.com**) and now on ScotlandsPeople (Chapter 1).

The project's cataloguing efforts saw the holdings of more than fifty archives documented, which can be accessed through the site and directly at **https://catalogue.nrscotland.gov.uk/scancatalogue/welcome. aspx**. While the SCAN project offers a single access point for researchers to search collections across Scotland, it is important to remember that the project ceased its work in 2004, and has not been updated since then. Many archives now have their own online catalogues, and so these should also be consulted if available.

Further centralised searches can be performed at the Archives Hub (**https://archiveshub.jisc.ac.uk**), representing collections from 220 academic institutions across the UK.

## The National Archives (TNA)
**www.nationalarchives.gov.uk**
Located near London at Kew, the UK's National Archives acts primarily as a national repository for England and Wales, but also holds a great deal of documentation for Scotland and Northern Ireland within its various British record sets, as well as some holdings specifically relevant to each territory.

Scotland is also included within various British collections of relevance, such as military records, civil service records, material from the Scottish Office, passenger records, holdings of the Board of Trade and naturalisation papers. As many Scots also moved to England and Wales, collections from these regions may be of considerable use, including probate records and the southern UK censuses. The archive's website contains research and resources guides, as well as a phenomenal amount of digitised material, accessible through its 'Discovery' catalogue (**https://discovery.nationalarchives.gov.uk**).

Holdings for many English and Welsh county-based archives and other repositories are included within TNA's Discovery catalogue. This also includes some entries for Scottish-based holdings, with search results providing links to the relevant archive catalogue. Previously known as ARCHON, the site's 'Find an archive in the UK and beyond' page at **https://discovery.nationalarchives.gov.uk/find-an-archive** can also help with contact details and web links for specific archives. Private holdings documented by the UK National Register of Archives are also included within Discovery.

The archive hosts an extensive collection of research guides at **www.nationalarchives.gov.uk/help-with-your-research/research-guides-keywords/**, many of them specific to topics of relevance to England and Wales only. Among its guides on British topics are the exceptionally useful military resources.

TNA is by far the most pro-active archive in the UK in terms of its efforts to digitise its holdings, the agency having formed partnerships with commercial bodies such as Ancestry, FindmyPast and TheGenealogist, as well as FamilySearch. These commercial bodies are discussed further on p.16, while many of TNA's digitised resources will be referred to throughout this book. The archive also has a dedicated gateway page to its digitised records at **www.nationalarchives.gov.uk/help-with-your-research/research-guides**. This provides links to collections available only from the archive's website, but also identifies which commercial companies host its other holdings. Not all of its digital records are keyword searchable, with a range of free-to-access digital microfilms available at **www.nationalarchives.gov.uk/help-with-your-research/research-guides/free-online-records-digital-microfilm/** which must be browsed.

## The National Library of Scotland (NLS) *Leabharlann Nàiseanta na h-Alba*
**www.nls.uk**

The National Library of Scotland (NLS) is Scotland's only legal deposit library. As both a national resource and one of the major research libraries in Europe, it offers free access to millions of items. The NLS has undertaken a massively ambitious project to digitise a full third of all of its holdings by 2025 for global access, although this includes digital materials that it will continue to receive via legal deposit. The target also includes a substantial amount of material from its historic holdings, much of which is already available online.

The library's website offers a handy guide to getting under way with family history research at **www.nls.uk/family-history**. In terms of documentary resources, the institution also offers several main areas of interest accessible from the home page. From the main menu, the 'Using the Library' option leads to a page with various guides to visiting the repository, as well as information on library cards, group tours and the various NLS buildings. If you scroll down there is a page entitled 'Catalogues & databases', which hosts various useful tools for research. These include the 'Library Search' catalogue, the 'Manuscripts catalogues and databases', a 'Guide to Scottish newspaper indexes' (p.66), and the various 'Scots Abroad' databases, for information on published accounts of emigrants to North America and Australasia. Additional tools include the 'Scottish song index', the 'Scottish Bibliographies Online' resource, and the 'Scottish theatre programmes database'.

The NLS's Moving Image catalogue (**https://movingimage.nls.uk**) provides over 2,000 clips and full-length Scottish films online, as sourced from the much larger Moving Image Archive (**www.nls.uk/collections/moving-image-archive**). This contains over 46,000 items, as well as off-air recordings of all Gaelic television broadcasts made in Scotland since 1993.

The 'Digital Resources' section (**www.nls.uk/digital-resources**) is where the NLS's main digital holdings are to be found. It includes the following categories:

### Digital gallery

This section contains a whole host of resources, the full list of which is accessible by clicking on the 'Show All in A-Z Order' link, or within a variety of categories, as follows: Art & design, Family history, Films, Kings & queens, Learning, Literature & writers, Maps & mapping, Medieval manuscripts, Music & song, Photography, Poetry, Printing & publishing, Religion & religious texts, Science & natural history, Scottish history & people, Scottish places, Social history, Sport, Theatre, Travel & emigration, and War.

Within the family history category, for example, there are a variety of publications of genealogical value, including a *Biographical dictionary of eminent Scotsmen*, *British military lists*, *Genealogical collections concerning families in Scotland 1750–1751*, *Rolls of honour*, and *Scottish Post Office Directories*, among many others.

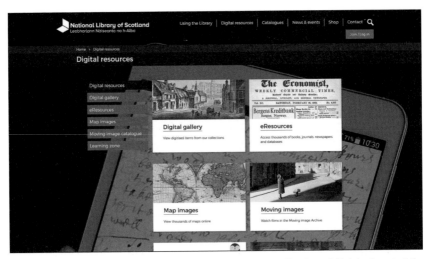

*The NLS Digital Resources page hosts an ever-growing collection of digitised materials.*

Note that many of the collections available here are also available on the Internet Archive's website at **https://archive.org/details/national libraryofscotland**, it being a key partner of the NLS in its digitisation efforts. In some cases, there are in fact materials available through the Internet Archive not available on the NLS site, such as post-1911 Scottish Post Office Directories (p.59).

### eResources
The NLS allows users with Scottish-based addresses to register on the site to gain free access to additional third-party databases and resources, some of which when accessed separately are subscription-based, or available through subscribing institutions only.

Once registered, you will be able to access various important databases, and to store those that are of most interest to you within a 'My resources' section, to help ease their location in future visits. Among the resources available are many newspaper collections (p.66), the UK Parliamentary Papers website, *Who's Who* and *Who Was Who*, the *Oxford Dictionary of National Biography*, and various ebook platforms. (Note that many other libraries and institutions across Scotland, the UK and worldwide offer similar access to such collections, available by free registration).

### Map images
This leads to the NLS's dedicated mapping platform at **https://maps.nls. uk**, which will be discussed further on p.63.

*Moving image catalogue*
This link leads to the Moving Image Archive as discussed earlier.

*Learning Zone*
The NLS offers many useful learning aids to help with the curriculum for Scottish schools.

There is quite a bit of replication on the NLS website, in terms of menu options for certain collections. Many of the NLS's searchable catalogues already described can also be found through the home page's main menu, through its 'Catalogues' option. A particularly useful category here is the 'Archives & manuscripts' page, which offers advice and information about materials available for consultation in the library's Special Collections Reading Room.

## Other libraries

The Scottish Library and Information Council has a Find a Library map at **https://scottishlibraries.org/find-a-library**. This can help you to locate contact details for libraries across the country, including local authority-run services, higher education-based resources, and specialist libraries, such as the Library of Innerpeffray (**www.innerpeffraylibrary.co.uk**) at Crieff, the first free public lending library in the country, founded in 1680 by David Drummond, 3rd Lord Madertie.

One of the largest public reference libraries in Europe is the Mitchell Library in Glasgow (**www.glasgowlife.org.uk/libraries/venues/the-mitchell-library**), which houses the city's archives, as well as many collections of national significance. The library's 'Family History at the Mitchell' service at **www.glasgowfamilyhistory.org.uk** notes details of how the city archive, the Glasgow registrars' service and the library itself can assist with your research.

The Glasgow Women's Library (**https://womenslibrary.org.uk**) is a national library, archive and museum dedicated to celebrating the lives, histories and achievements of women, with collections as diverse as Suffragette memorabilia and 1930s dressmaking patterns to *Scottish Women's Liberation* newsletters from the 1970s. The organisation's website hosts a variety of resources, including a searchable online catalogue for the holdings of its lending library, and its 'LGBTQ Collections Online Resource' hosting digitised materials from its Lesbian Archive and LGBTQ collections.

Many academic libraries from learning institutions across Scotland will allow public access. A list of such libraries, which are members of the

Scottish Confederation of University and Research Libraries (SCURL), is available at **https://scurl.ac.uk/who-we-are/scurl-members/**.

The British Library in London holds millions of books, journals, patents, sound recordings and more. Its website (**www.bl.uk**) hosts several online exhibitions, catalogues and digitised examples from its holdings, and several dedicated sites for particular collections such as its newspaper holdings or its Indian records holdings, some of which require a subscription. Useful pages to bookmark include the Help for Researchers section at **www.bl.uk/catalogues-and-collections**, which lists all of the facility's online catalogues, including its main library catalogue, its Sound and Moving Image Catalogue, and the British National Biography site (**https://bnb.bl.uk**), which lists all books and journals published or distributed in the UK and Ireland since 1950.

A further essential platform for locating items of interest within Scottish libraries, and further afield, is WorldCat (**www.worldcat.org**).

## Historic Environment Scotland *Àrainneachd Eachdraidheil Alba*
**www.historicenvironment.scot**
Historic Environment Scotland (HES) is the main heritage body for the country, and was formed in 2015 from a merger of Historic Scotland and the Royal Commission on the Ancient and Historical Manuscripts of Scotland. Its website offers access to various resources through its Archives and Research page, including the following:

### *National Collection of Aerial Photography (NCAP)*
This site at **https://ncap.org.uk** hosts more than 1.6 million images of Scotland, in a collection totalling 26 million photos.

### *HLAmap*
The Historic Land-Use Assessment Project at **https://hlamap.org.uk** allows users to compare the modern use of Scotland's land with the historic environment.

### *Canmore*
This database is accessed via **https://canmore.org.uk** and allows users to find archaeological and heritage-based information on some 300,000 historical places in Scotland. The MyCanmore section of the platform also allows users to contribute their own material, making it a truly interactive repository.

## Britain from Above
This site at **www.britainfromabove.org.uk** holds aerial images taken from 1919–1953.

## ScotlandsPlaces
Available at **www.scotlandsplaces.gov.uk**, this is a joint project between HES, the NRS and the NLI, and offers a variety of useful records and resources.

## SCRAN
The Scottish Cultural Resource Network offers access to over 490,000 images, sounds and videos from over 300 museums, archives and galleries in Scotland, through a subscription-based platform at **www.scran.ac.uk**.

## PastMap
An interactive online map to locate Scotland's archaeological and historic sites. Its holdings include scheduled monuments, conservation areas, battlefields and gardens and designed landscapes. It can be accessed at **https://pastmap.org.uk**.

## Buildings at Risk Register
Searchable by local authority area, this site at **www.buildingsatrisk.org.uk** documents important and historic sites considered to be at risk.

## Family and Local History Societies
The majority of genealogical societies across Scotland are members of the Scottish Association of Family History Societies (SAFHS). Its website at **www.safhs.org.uk** provides details of each group, as well as useful databases on the locations of burial grounds across Scotland and pre-1841 population lists. The site's 'Bulletins' section also provides society news twice yearly from across the country, while the organisation's Facebook page offers further family history news and developments.

The Edinburgh-based Scottish Genealogy Society at **www.scotsgenealogy.com** has an online 'Family History Index' outlining some of the private papers which have been deposited with the body, as well as a downloadable index for its journal *The Scottish Genealogist* from 1953–2005. The 'Downloads' section also hosts *The Black Book*, detailing all of the society's holdings relating to Scottish deaths and burials, arranged by county and in downloadable PDF format. The majority are for Scottish counties, but there are listings for the English border counties of Cumbria and Northumberland. The society has a Facebook page at **www.facebook.com/ScottishGenealogySociety**.

A separate organisation is that of the University of the Third Age (U3A), which offers a range of self-help learning opportunities for retired and semi-retired people. A list of U3A members' groups across Scotland is available at **https://u3asites.org.uk/scotland/members**, offering a range of activities including opportunities for 'Family History' or 'Genealogy'. Members offer mutual support for research efforts, and many groups have regular talks programmes on topics of ancestral themes.

Various other family history societies beyond Scotland may also hold materials of interest. The Anglo-Scottish Family History Society was formed in 1982 by members of the Manchester and Lancashire Family History Society, and has a dedicated page on its website at **https://angloscots.mlfhs.org.uk**. It offers the Scottish Marriage Index at **https://angloscots.mlfhs.org.uk/smi/smi.php**, documenting marriages where at least one of the spouses is Scots born. The details of many other societies in England and Wales can be found through the Family History Federation at **www.familyhistoryfederation.com**.

Additional bodies include the Catholic Family History Society (**https://catholicfhs.online**), the Guild of One-Name Studies (**https://one-name.org**) and the International Society for British Genealogy and Family History (**https://isbgfh.com**). Another useful resource for research into Scottish ancestors is the Families in British India Society (**www.fibis.org**), which has a substantial number of free-to-access databases on its website, as well as members-only holdings.

In the Western Isles, historical societies known in Gaelic as '*comainn eachdraidh*' exist independently to the family history societies on the mainland. A general list of those known to exist and with active websites has been provided online by the Gaelic college Sabhal Mòr Ostaig at **www.smo.uhi.ac.uk/gaidhlig/buidhnean/eachdraidh**, with a further listing at **www.hebrideanconnections.com**. Most society sites have some online resources, although they vary considerably.

The Scottish Local History Forum (**www.slhf.org**) is the main umbrella body for local history societies in Scotland. Its website provides details of the organisation, including the latest news and events, but its 'SLH Directory' page at **www.slhf.org/scottish-local-history-directory**, which hosts its 'Scottish Local History Directory', is particularly worth bookmarking. This provides details of many resources and organisations across the country holding them, which may be useful for your research. Some sample articles from its journal, *Scottish Local History*, can also be read, with an online index provided to help trace additional articles.

The Local History Online platform at **www.local-history.co.uk** includes further details of Scottish history societies.

## Commercial vendors and services

There are many commercial vendors digitising Scottish and additional British resources which document the lives of our forebears, with the family history market increasingly competitive. Some offer subscriptions and/or pay-per-view credits, while others offer look-up services for records to which they have created indexes.

When subscribing to sites, note that some offer an introductory period for free, which you will need to register for with your credit card details. Do be aware of their terms and conditions for use, particularly if you work as a professional genealogist. Also note that some vendors take credit card details when you register and at the end of the free period 'automatically renew' your subscription. Check to see if there is a tick box that allows you to stop this from happening, or make sure that you cancel your subscription before the renewal period approaches, if you do not wish for a lump sum to suddenly disappear from your bank account! It is also worth signing up to the newsletters and social media platforms of many of the sites, for news of free access periods to certain collections.

The following are the largest platforms with significant offerings of Scottish interest, which will be constantly referred to throughout this book.

### Ancestry
**www.ancestry.co.uk**

Ancestry.co.uk is the UK's platform for the American-based Ancestry.com corporation, which has various web domains offering access to its collections across the world. The site offers access to its resources either by a monthly or annual subscription, or through a pay-as-you-go model.

To locate the most relevant collections for Scotland use the 'Search' tab on the main menu, and then consult the site's 'Card Catalogue', which can be searched for by collection name or by keyword. Alternatively, visit the 'Search all records' option under the 'Search' tab, and then use the 'Explore by Location' map function on the page returned, selecting 'Scotland' as the country of interest. Once done, Ancestry will return a list of both Scottish and UK-based resources, with the collection title, the category under which it will be found, and the number of records within the record set.

Among some of the most useful unique Scottish resources on the site are the following:

- Glasgow, Scotland, Crew Lists, 1863–1901
- Perthshire, Scotland, Cess, Stent and Valuation Rolls, 1650–1899
- Scottish Covenanters Index
- Muthill, Perthshire, Scotland, Register of Baptisms, 1697–1847
- Perth, Scotland, Register of Deeds, 1566–1811
- Directory of Scottish Settlers in North America, 1625–1825. Vol. I
- Scots in the West Indies, 1707–1857
- Scotland, The Register of The Privy Council of Scotland, 1545–1632
- Scotland, The Register of the Great Seal of Scotland, 1306–1651
- *Fasti Ecclesiae Scoticanae*. The succession of ministers in the parish churches of Scotland
- Scotland, National Probate Index (Calendar of Confirmations and Inventories), 1876–1936
- Perth and Kinross, Scotland, Electoral Registers, 1832–1961
- Fife, Scotland, School Admissions and Discharges, 1867–1916
- Rosyth, Fife, Scotland, Dockyard Employee Books, 1892–1967
- Fife, Scotland, Electoral Registers, 1914–1966
- Aberdeen City and Former Counties of Aberdeenshire, Scotland, Electoral Registers, 1832–1976

There are many additional UK-themed collections that are equally as valuable, including its military records collections and occupational records sets, which will be discussed in Chapter 4.

In certain collections on Ancestry the results returned will be comprised of several documents, but the page you first arrive at may not necessarily be the first in the particular batch concerning the person of interest. This is because they may not have been in the correct order when they were microfilmed and then digitised. If possible, remember to browse the pages before the one you land on, as well as those after. This is particularly true for its First World War service records and some of its merchant navy holdings.

Ancestry offers a tree-building facility, and if you have an Apple or Android-based computer tablet or phone you can download a free app that allows you to sync your tree on your device to your main Ancestry account on a PC or Mac (see **www.ancestry.co.uk/cs/ancestry-app**). The platform also offers an online collaboration tool called the 'World Archives Project', which allows the company to 'crowd source' collections, with volunteers indexing digitised collections. Additional services include print publishing facilities for books, tree charts and posters. Ancestry DNA at **www.ancestry.co.uk/dna** is also one of the most powerful genealogical research tools available for tracing genetic cousins (p.71).

Ancestry has several social media outlets to keep you up to date with new releases, including Twitter at @ancestryUK, Facebook at **www.facebook.com/AncestryUK** and a blog at **https://blogs.ancestry.com/ancestry**.

## FindmyPast
**www.findmypast.co.uk**
FindmyPast originally started in the UK as a site offering indexes to civil registration records for English and Welsh births, marriages and deaths from 1837 onwards, and which later expanded to offer British census records and parish records. Today the site has several worldwide platforms, including FindmyPast Ireland (**www.findmypast.ie**), FindmyPast Australasia (**www.findmypast.com.au**) and the US-based FindmyPast (**www.findmypast.com**).

Although each worldwide site started off with very different offerings, their records are now collectively accessible through each platform, by various subscription means. This means that while Scottish and British records can be easily searched through all the platforms, it is also possible to search for Scottish emigrants who made lives in overseas territories.

The key holdings of FindmyPast are arranged within the following categories:

- Census, land & substitutes
- Directories & social history
- Immigration & travel
- Life events (birth, marriage, death)
- Newspapers & periodicals
- Churches & religion
- Education & work
- Institutions & organisations
- Military service & conflict

Many of the Scottish datasets are in fact third-party indexes or transcriptions of collections supplied by family history societies and companies such as Scottish Monumental Inscriptions, Scottish Indexes, Old Scottish, and the Scottish Genealogy Society. Among the collections uniquely hosted by FindmyPast are the following:

- Scotland, Linlithgowshire (West Lothian), Electoral Registers 1864–1931
- Scotland, Post Office Directories
- Scotland, University of St Andrews Matriculations 1747–1897
- Scotland, Scottish Peerages

FindmyPast also offers its own transcriptions of the 1841–1901 Scottish censuses (p.57), and, as with Ancestry, hosts many UK-themed resources which are equally useful for researching Scots.

A global search facility across all collections is available, along with an A-Z listing, FindmyPast also has a partnership with LivingDNA to offer DNA tests (p.73), and hosts the largest collection of Scottish Roman Catholic records, as sourced from the Scottish Catholic Archives.

The company also has a regularly updated blog at **www.findmypast.co.uk/blog**, and has accounts for Facebook at **www.facebook.com/findmypast** and Twitter at @findmypast. A tree-building programme is freely available on the site at **www.findmypast.co.uk/family-tree/create**

### Scottish Indexes
**www.scottishindexes.com**
Scottish Indexes offers a valuable finding aid to many NRS holdings, as well as a look-up service for the records indexed.

The site's holdings can be searched through the 'Advanced Search' section on the home page menu, or through individual search pages for each collection, accessible through the 'Record Sets' tab. They are arranged into the following categories:

- Mental Health Records
- Scotland's Criminal Database
- Scottish Paternity Index

*Scottish Indexes, from Graham and Emma Maxwell, offers a pathway to many previously unindexed NRS records.*

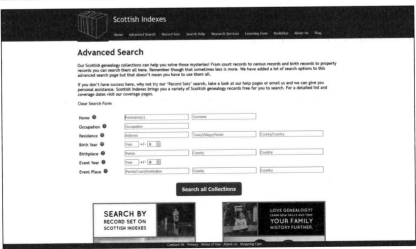

- Register of Deeds
- Register of Sasines
- Kelso Dispensary Patient Registers
- Non-OPR Births/Baptisms
- Non-OPR Banns/Marriages
- Non-OPR Deaths/Burials
- Pre-1841 Censuses and Population Lists
- 1841 Census
- 1851 Census
- 1861 Census

The census records are full transcriptions for households in the southern counties of Scotland, and are completely free to view.

The site's indexes are also free to consult, offering some limited details from the records and their relevant accession numbers from the archive; this means that you can in fact use the site as a catalogue, and upon locating a record of interest, consult it at the NRS in Edinburgh yourself. However, if you cannot easily get to the archive, you can request a copy of the record from the team, which you can pay for through PayPal.

The site also offers some useful information about its various record sets, which can be read within the 'Learning Zone' section.

### Old Scottish Genealogy & Family History
**www.oldscottish.com**

Old Scottish offers a similar service to Scottish Indexes, with indexes to various collections held at the NRS. These can be searched through the category listings on the home page, or through the 'Records' tab of the menu on the home page.

Among the resources available to search through the site are the following:

- General Register of Lunatics in Asylums
- Sheriff Court affiliation and aliment decrees
- Scottish school leaving certificates and exam results.
- Registers of the Inspector of Anatomy for Scotland, 1842–1949
- Rolls of Male Heads of Families 1834–1842
- Kirk Session minutes
- Poor Law appeals to the Board of Supervision
- Records of births with no father named (1855–1874)

Many of the records can be located by county and parish. Some limited information is made freely available, while copies of full records can be purchased.

The site also offers a blog, and an online shop where you can purchase PDF-based publications of many resources, including dissenting Presbyterian church records.

## TheGenealogist
**www.thegenealogist.co.uk**

Scottish records on TheGenealogist are somewhat limited, comprised mainly of a number of trade directories, part of the 1851 census, and landowner records from 1872–1873, all of which are oddly listed in the 'Scottish Records' category in its 'International' section. A small number of additional Scottish holdings are also available in other categories, such as Aberdeenshire-based parish records in its 'Parish Transcript Baptisms' category.

As with Ancestry and FindmyPast, TheGenealogist offers many British collections from TNA and other agencies, with the most useful categories for Scottish research being as follows:

- Births, Marriages & Deaths (including overseas UK BMDs)
- Immigration, Emigration and Travel
- Military Records
- Non-Conformist Records

The last collection here is also hosted by the firm on a completely separate website, BMD Registers at **www.bmdregisters.com**, and holds the following collections of vital records from TNA, many of which will include Scots in England, based overseas, or at sea:

- RG4: Non-parochial Registers 1567–1858
- RG5: Protestant Dissenters' Registry
- RG6: Quaker Registers 1578–1841
- RG7: Fleet Marriages 1667–1777
- RG8: Non-Parochial & Miscellaneous Registers
- RG32: Registers Abroad and on British & Foreign Ships 1831–1969
- RG33: Foreign Registers & Returns 1627–1960
- RG34: Worldwide Foreign Marriage Returns 1826–1921
- RG35: General Register Office: Miscellaneous Foreign Death Returns – 1791–1921
- RG36: Registers & Returns in the Protectorates etc of Africa & Asia

- BT158: Registers compiled from Ships' Official Logs of passengers at sea 1854–1908
- BT159: Registers of Deaths at sea of British and other nationalities
- 1875–1888
- BT160: Registers of Births at sea of British Nationals 1875–1891

The site offers various subscription levels, and has its own free tree-building software platform, called TreeView (also available at **www. treeview.co.uk**).

### Forces War Records
**www.forces-war-records.co.uk**
Forces War Records is a subscription-based military records platform that has various rolls of honour, medal rolls and other useful military materials. Free offerings include a series of photo galleries from both world wars, and some handy research guides.

While the site has many collections that are also available on sites such as Ancestry and FindmyPast, it equally has several unique collections of interest to those researching Scots in the military. These include:

- British & Imperial Prisoners of War Held by Japan WWII
- Home Guard Officer Lists 1939–45
- Home Guard Auxiliary Units Roll WWII
- British & Imperial Prisoners of War held in Italy WWII
- Military Hospitals Admissions and Discharge Registers WWI
- Royal Artillery 1877–81
- Territorial Force Nursing Service Medal Rolls
- The Seventeenth Highland Light Infantry 1914
- The Union Bank of Scotland Ltd Roll of honour 1914–1918

Also available are lists taken from the muster rolls of the Scottish (or North British) Militia at the start of 1800 (catalogued under WO13 at TNA), and from the two Scottish battalions (5th and 14th) of the Army Reserve just prior to 1805 (as sourced from WO12).

### Deceased Online
**www.deceasedonline.com**
Deceased Online commenced operations in 2008 and offers access to many digitised burial and cremation records from across Britain, as well as cemetery maps in many cases. Scottish material includes burials from Aberdeen City and Aberdeenshire, and Edinburgh Crematorium, as well

as access to many Scottish gravestone inscriptions, as supplied from Scottish Monumental Inscriptions (p.53). The site also offers various military burial records, as sourced from TNA, both in England and overseas.

Searches are free, but credits need to be purchased to view the full result. Information on funeral applicants within the last seventy-five years is restricted for data protection reasons.

*FamilySearch*
**www.familysearch.org**
FamilySearch is the free online records site of the Church of Jesus Christ of Latter-Day Saints. The site has partnered with Ancestry and FindmyPast on many projects, and will be discussed throughout this book.

*MyHeritage*
**www.myheritage.com**
MyHeritage is an Israel-based platform with limited databases of use for Scottish research, but with a very impressive DNA platform (p.73).

## Professional researchers

In addition to online vendors, you may wish to seek help from professional researchers. Among those who may be able to help are members of the Association of Professional Genealogists (**www. apgen.org**), the Association of Scottish Genealogists and Researchers in Archives (**www.asgra.co.uk**), and the Scottish Genealogy Network (**https://scottishgenealogynetwork.blogspot.com**).

Note that many local authorities across the country will also offer research services, as will some family history societies.

## Online Family History Courses

Two Scottish universities offer postgraduate-level family history qualifications which are taught entirely online. The University of Strathclyde offers a Postgraduate Certificate, Diploma or MSc in Genealogical Studies, with details available at **www.strath.ac.uk/ studywithus/centreforlifelonglearning/genealogy/**. In addition it also runs regular free online 'MOOC' courses (Massive Open Online Course) and a series of short eight-week beginners to intermediate level genealogy courses. The University of Dundee runs a separate postgraduate MLitt Family and Local History course, with details at **www.dundee.ac.uk/ study/pg/family-local-history/**, which can also be studied at MSc, Diploma or Certificate level.

On the Isle of Skye, the Gaelic college Sabhal Mòr Ostaig (part of the University of the Highlands and Islands) offers an optional Genealogy module as part of its Dip HE Gaelic and Related Studies course, which can be studied via distance learning – details are available at **www.smo. uhi.ac.uk/en/cursaichean/dioploma-he-gaidhlig-is-cuspairean-co-cheangailte**.

If you wish to study in a more leisurely fashion, other shorter courses are available. The University of Glasgow teaches an online Early Modern Scottish Palaeography: Reading Scotland's Records course, with details accessible via **www.nrscotland.gov.uk/research/learning/palaeography**, while the NRS also offers its own palaeography tuition site (p.6).

Pharos Teaching and Tutoring Limited (**www.pharostutors.com**) offers two Scottish courses, Scottish Research Online and Scotland 1750–1850: Beyond the OPRs, both originally written by genealogist Sherry Irvine, and currently taught by yours truly.

The Scottish Genealogy Society also offers a series of workshops throughout the year, with details accessible from its home page (under the 'Home' menu option).

## Networking and Communication

A problem shared is a problem halved, and one of the best ways to seek advice for a genealogical brick wall issue is to collaborate over a research problem through one of many different online platforms, including discussion forums, social media, online family tree collaboration, and by other means.

### Tree Building

Many free family tree-building programmes can be found online, such as TreeView (**www.treeview.co.uk**), Tribal Pages (**www.tribalpages. com**) or Heredis (**www.heredis.com/en**), while commercial vendors such as Ancestry, FindmyPast and MyHeritage (**www.myheritage.com**) offer basic tree-building services with many additional features that can be pursued by a subscription. Using such sites you can search in other people's trees for possible connections, and contact them if you find a match with your own.

### Discussion Forums

TalkingScot offers a free to access dedicated Scottish-based discussion platform at **www.talkingscot.com**. The home page of the site is well worth bookmarking, as it offers a range of useful resources, including lists of family history societies active in Scotland, libraries, and a useful section on Scotland's censuses. The main forum itself has four main discussion areas, the key sections being the 'TalkingScot Forum' and 'Scots Abroad'.

RootsChat (**www.rootschat.com**) is a much larger platform covering Britain and Ireland, with Scotland well catered for in three main areas. By far the largest is the main 'Scotland' posting area, where you can post enquiries and questions not limited to a particular county, or within a sub-category for a county. The smaller 'Scotland Resources' category offers suggestions for various helpful resources for research both offline and online, while the 'Gaelic Language' section allows you to post queries using Scottish Gaelic (p.27). This should not be confused with the separate section for Irish Gaelic (Gaeilge), which is listed as 'Irish Language'.

Ancestry's RootsWeb platform is one of the oldest forums around, having been first established in 1993. It hosts some 25 million posts on topics hosted on almost 200,000 separate 'message boards', accessible at **https://home.rootsweb.com** or through Ancestry's home page under the 'Help' topic. There are various ways to locate boards of potential interest, including a keyword search facility, and searches for boards by surname or by locality. Scotland and Scottish surnames are well represented, and once you have found a particular message board of interest you can further narrow down your search within it using additional keywords.

Other forums which exist include those run by family history magazines (p.26), while several family history societies (p.14) also have dedicated areas for members to discuss their interests. For military

*The Rootschat discussion forum has many members willing to cooperate with family history enquiries.*

matters, one of the best resources is the Great War Forum at **www. greatwarforum.org**, which covers just about every military topic that you may wish to discuss for the First World War.

### Social Media

Various social media-based networking platforms can also help with collaboration. On Facebook (**www.facebook.com**) you will find many Scottish community-based groups, while Twitter (**https://twitter.com**) allows users to 'tweet' short messages of up to 280 characters in length, through what is termed 'micro-blogging'. You will find the Twitter address at **@genesblog**, for example, where I regularly comment on family history developments, as well as provide occasional 'retweets' of other people's announcements from accounts that I follow.

I also use Facebook and Twitter to provide links to posts on my blog site, Scottish GENES (**https://scottishgenes.blogspot.com**), on which I carry details of various family history events and developments from Scotland and across Britain and Ireland, including new records releases online. There are many blogs available online of Scottish interest from archives, libraries and commercial services, including 'Scottish Genealogy Tips and Tidbits' at **https://scottishgenealogytipsntricks.blogspot.com** from Canadian Scot Christine Woodcock, and one of my faves, 'Orkney Archive – Get Dusty', at **https://orkneyarchive.blogspot.com**, which treads a fine line between sheer brilliance and utter irreverence!

Various platforms allow you to network by sharing photos and images, include Pinterest (**www.pinterest.co.uk**) and Instagram (**www. instagram.com**). For videos of Scottish interest, search on YouTube (**www.youtube.com**) and Vimeo (**https://vimeo.com**).

Other social networking sites which allow you to collaborate include Curious Fox (**https://curiousfox.com**), which allows connections to be made by village or town names, or Peter Calver's Lost Cousins (**www. lostcousins.com**), which facilitates the establishment of connections by the use of census information – pop your relative's census details in, and if someone else does the same, you can establish if your families are related. Peter's regular family history newsletter is also well worth subscribing to on the site.

### Magazines

The print magazines *Family Tree* (**https://family-tree.co.uk**) and *Who Do You Think You Are* (**www.whodoyouthinkyouaremagazine.com**) occasionally cover Scottish topics, as well as regular news and discussion forums, with digital versions of both titles also available online.

*Discover Your Ancestors* is another monthly magazine which exists in digital format only, available from **https://discoveryourancestors.co.uk**, which also features occasional topics of Scottish interest.

## Languages and Handwriting

Historically, the three main languages spoken in Scotland in the recorded period have been English, Scots, and Gaelic (Gàidhlig), with many earlier records also written exclusively in Latin (or worse – Scottish legal Latin!). Various place names across the country also testify to much older tongues once in use, such as Pictish and Norn (an evolution of Old Norse as spoken in Orkney and Shetland).

While English is universally spoken today across Scotland, Scots is still spoken in most parts to a degree across the country, with strong dialects such as Doric still present in the north-east. The Scots Language Centre (Centre for the Scots Leid) also offers a range of background resources for the language at **www.scotslanguage.com**.

From a family history perspective, while the language of spoken Scots today is heavily impacted on by the mainly English-language media, as you go further back in time through historic records the language becomes a considerably more difficult challenge to overcome, with many words and grammatical constructs no longer in use. By far the most useful resource for understanding older Scots words is the free to access Dictionary of the Scots Language (Dictionar o the Scots Leid), available at **https://dsl.ac.uk**. The SCAN website's Glossary can help with both Scots and Latin-derived legal terms at **www.scan.org.uk/ researchrtools/glossary.htm**, with further assistance available from the Scottish Law Online website at **www.scottishlaw.org.uk/lawscotland/ abscotslawland.html**.

A commonly quoted phrase in Scottish genealogy is the Gaelic *'cuimhnich air na daoine o'n d' thàinig thu'* ('remember those from whom you came'). Gaelic (Gàidhlig) shares a strong connection with the Irish language (Gaeilge) and Manx (Gaelg or Gailck), with all three being modern evolved variants of an older common Goidelic language (Middle Irish). A handy online tool is Google Translate, available at **https:// translate.google.co.uk**, but should you wish to learn the language, the BBC's online TV series from 1979, *Can Seo*, is a great resource available on YouTube, while BBC Alba (**www.bbc.com/alba**) regularly broadcasts each night in the language, and daily via Radio nan Gaidheal. Additional learning resources can be found at **https://learngaelic.scot**, including the very handy Litir do Luchd-Ionnsachaidh (Letter to Learners) section for more advanced learners, and Duolingo, via **www.duolingo.com**.

Many surnames in Scotland are derived from Gaelic; Sabhal Mòr Ostaig hosts a page at **www.smo.uhi.ac.uk/gaidhlig/ainmean/sloinnidhean. html** detailing a handy list of English and Gaelic surname equivalents, with a corresponding page for forenames at **www.smo.uhi.ac.uk/gaidhlig/ ainmean/ainmean.html**.

The University of Edinburgh-funded Tobar an Dualchais/A Kist o Riches website at **www.tobarandualchais.co.uk** hosts some 50,000 recordings of stories, songs, music and poetry in both Gaelic and Scots, as recorded since the 1930s, which have been sourced from the School of Scottish Studies (University of Edinburgh), BBC Scotland and the National Trust for Scotland's Canna Collection.

In addition to language issues, another real barrier that will present itself the further back you go with your Scottish research is the issue of handwriting, with older forms of writing such as Secretary Hand providing some real challenges – particularly when combined with an increasing frequency of older Scots words.

The NRS has a dedicated platform called Scottish Handwriting at **www.scottishhandwriting.com**, which is designed to help users learn how to read older forms of letters and words. The site provides an overview of the basics of palaeography, and a series of tutorials and challenges to help improve your understanding of documents such as hearth tax rolls.

*The NRS Scottish Handwriting platform offers free tuition to help you learn the older form of writing known as 'Secretary Hand'.*

*Chapter 2*

# WHO WERE THEY? SCOTLANDSPEOPLE

By far the most important website for getting underway with Scottish ancestral research is the ScotlandsPeople records platform at **www. scotlandspeople.gov.uk**, administered by the NRS in Edinburgh. The site describes itself as 'the official Scottish Government site for searching government records and archives', and carries a variety of digitised records, as sourced from the NRS, the Scottish Catholic Archives (p.80) and the Court of the Lord Lyon (p.42). Most notably, it provides access to vital records, parish records, censuses, and wills and testaments.

One of the key things about ScotlandsPeople is that its records can be explored both at home, and at a series of research centres across Scotland. These currently include the ScotlandsPeople Centre in Edinburgh, the Glasgow Genealogy Centre at the Mitchell Library, the Burns Monument Centre at Kilmarnock, the Hawick Heritage Hub, the Highland Archive Service Family History Centre in Inverness, and Clackmannanshire Family History Centre in Alloa (details for all are available at **www.nrscotland.gov. uk/research/local-family-history-centres**). When accessing the database from one of these centres, the service offered is somewhat modified. Once you have registered an account with the site, you can use the same login details both at home and within a centre.

For domestic access, users are required to purchase a number of credits (at the time of writing charged at £7.50 for 30 credits), payable through the site using a credit or debit card, or PayPal. Any unused credits will remain available for up to two years, although the facility does occasionally offer 'amnesties' to restore unused credits that have expired. Alternatively, to use the ScotlandsPeople website at one of the centres, a statutory fee is paid for unlimited access to all records on a single day's visit (at the time of writing set at £15).

The biggest difference between the two forms of access is that there are various online closure periods for recent civil registration records, to prevent data mining and to protect privacy, whereas at the centres you can view civil registration records almost to the present day. If a record that has been indexed online falls within a closure period, a digital image will not be available, but an option will be provided to order a costlier certified extract, which will be posted to you.

A user's search history will be preserved, as will any records purchased. Saved images and searches can be consulted from menu options at the very top right of the home page, next to the user's account details.

## The home page

The home page of ScotlandsPeople offers menu options leading to various sections, while buttons to register an account and to log in are located to the top right of the screen. Registration is free, and a certain limited amount of information can be gained without cost through the online indexes. The real detail, however, is to be found within the hosted documents, which must be purchased for a certain number of credits. Additional sections of the home page provide the latest news from the ScotlandsPeople team, details about the nature of records held, and information about the ScotlandsPeople Centre in Edinburgh.

In the section entitled 'Find your Scottish ancestors', it is possible to do a search to gain a rough idea of how many records featuring a particular name are available on the site. However, the 'Search our records' menu option leads to the key part of the site, from where you can perform a more detailed exploration within the various record categories. On this page you will find three main areas offering information:

*Search for People* – this panel is the gateway to the main search screen for individual records collections.

*Search by Place* – this section provides access to information on place names and how to understand administrative boundaries, including a series of detailed 'county guides'.

*Image Library* – this section allows you to view well over 2,000 images grouped with a variety of categories, from Aerial Photography to World Cultures, which may be of interest for your research. Copies can also be purchased directly using a credit or debit card, or PayPal.

Each of these areas will now be explored in detail.

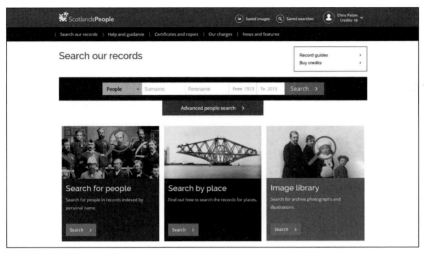

*The 'Search our records' page on ScotlandsPeople.*

## Search for People

The 'Search for People' section is where the Crown Jewels will be found, hosting the site's key records within six main categories, accessible through dedicated search pages and with a variety of fields available to help customise enquiries.

Beside the boxes for surnames and forenames are blue links entitled 'Search Options', which permit a number of ways to help control or widen a search, by looking for exact names only, by 'fuzzy matching', with wildcards allowed, by names beginning with a particular set of letters, with name variants, or by phonetic matching. The wildcards permitted are as follows:

For zero or more characters      * or %
For a single character only      ? or _

A guide to searching for forenames and surnames, and the search options available to do so, are available at **www.scotlandspeople.gov.uk/guides/ surnames** and **www.scotlandspeople.gov.uk/guides/forenames**.

Once an initial search is carried out, a series of filter options will become available for some of the collections on the left-hand side of the page; these will allow results to be narrowed down further, and in some cases even provide alternative ways to perform searches. It is also possible to reorder the presentation of results returned by clicking on the headings given at the top of the index entries. For example, they can be rearranged in chronological order, by order of age from youngest to oldest (or vice versa), or in alphabetical order of parents.

Some limited information is freely given in the returned index results, and the site permanently saves a history of searches for which images are purchased, as well as the images themselves, which can be accessed at any time from menu options at the top right of the screen. If a couple of years down the line you inadvertently repeat a search for which you purchased the record, instead of a box asking you to 'View Record', it will instead note 'Viewed (Paid)', and permit you to see the record again at no further cost. Records can also be placed into a timeline facility.

The six records categories are as follows, with some basic background given for each record set hosted:

### i) Statutory Registers

The statutory registration of births, marriages and deaths in Scotland commenced in January 1855, more than seventeen years after doing so south of the border. A useful account of how the system came into existence can be read online via the University of Glasgow's Scottish Way of Birth and Death platform at **www.gla.ac.uk/schools/socialpolitical/research/ economicsocialhistory/historymedicine/scottishwayofbirthanddeath/ introduction/**. My book *Tracing Your Scottish Ancestry Through Church and State Records* (p.168) also goes into considerably more detail on the legal requirements underpinning registration and the ancillary records generated (e.g. for vaccination).

Scotland's civil registration records more than make up for the system's late establishment by the sheer detail presented within each record. For example, you should in most records find the names of both parents to a newborn baby, to marrying spouses, and for a deceased person, meaning it is relatively easy to confirm that you have the correct John MacDonald in records from various stages throughout his life. The caveat to this is that such information, particularly with earlier records, is only as good as that submitted to a registrar by an informant, and only as good as the registrar's understanding of what has been said.

This section provides access to six record types:

*Births* – statutory birth records are available from 1855, but while they are indexed almost to the present day, images are only available online for records over 100 years old. The cost of an image is six credits.

The records offer the child's name, the sex, when and where born, the parents' names (and status), the father's occupation, the name of the informant, and when and where the event was registered. Prior to 1919 an illegitimate child will be so described under his or her name, and for most records, bar those from 1856–1860, the date and place of the parents' marriage will also be noted.

The registers for the year 1855 are particularly detailed, offering additional information on the parents' ages and birthplaces, the numbers of children produced by the parents to date, and with how many noted as still alive. For the year 1855 the indexes also contain the mother's maiden name. At family history centres providing access to ScotlandsPeople the indexes from 1929 onwards will offer the mother's maiden name also, although this facility is disabled for online access.

*Marriages* – statutory marriage records exist from 1855, with indexes online almost to the present day, but with a seventy-five-year closure period for more recent images. The cost of an image is six credits.

The records offer details of the date and location of the marriage (and minister and religious denomination if relevant, or the registrar from 1940 onwards), as well as the method of advance publication (banns prior to 1978, marriage notice from 1879 to the present day, or a Sheriff's license from 1940 to 1978), or whether an irregular marriage. For the two spouses, the information noted is their names, ages, occupations, status (bachelor, widow etc), their addresses and parents, including the fathers' occupations and whether still alive. In addition are the names of witnesses, the date of registration, and for regular marriages prior to 1940, the name of the celebrant.

Unlike the south of Britain, irregular marriage was perfectly legal in Scotland prior to 1940, requiring the couple to merely exchange consent before witnesses, and with no celebrant required. Such marriages will be apparent in the records, as a warrant had to be first granted by the Sheriff-Substitute for them to be registered, which will be noted.

For the year 1855 only, the records also note the birthplace of each partner, the number of previous marriages for each, and the number of children produced from such marriages.

*Divorces* – this offers the index to the statutory Register of Divorces from 1 May 1984 onwards, providing the names of the divorcing spouses, their date and place of marriage, the year of decree of divorce, and information on the Sheriff Court responsible. While the index is free, the images cannot be viewed online or at a family history centre, due to privacy concerns.

*Deaths* – statutory death records exist from 1855 onwards, and are indexed almost to the present day, although images are only available online for records over fifty years old. The cost of an image is six credits.

Death records note the name of the deceased and their status (married, widowed etc), along with the names of any spouses (not recorded from 1856–1860), plus information about their date, time and place of death, as well as their usual residence if not at home. As with birth and marriage records, the records also note the names of the deceased's parents.

Of all three record types, death records can be the least reliable at times, with the deceased having no say in the information offered – it is not unknown, for example, for an informant to provide the names of the wrong grandparents. The causes of death are also supplied, details of the informant, and where and when registered.

For the year 1855, death records also note the place of the deceased's burial, the name of the undertaker responsible, and the names of any children born to them, their names and ages, and if they died prior to 1855, their dates of death. The burial information continued to be recorded until 1860.

*Civil partnerships* – a database of indexes for Scottish civil partnerships from 5 December 2005 onwards. The images are not online, but copies can be ordered as certified extracts.

*Dissolutions* – a database noting the dissolutions of Scottish civil partnerships from 5 December 2005 onwards.

In addition to the above, a record may have a margin note to the immediate left of the entry concerned, advising the user to consult the Register of Corrected Entries (Register of Corrections from 1966). This will note changes that were subsequently recorded for registrations, to correct a mistake or to provide information subsequently obtained. For example, it might note the result of an investigation into an unusual or suspicious death by a procurator fiscal, or a court judgement concerning the decreed paternity of an illegitimate child.

Where such records are noted, they can be consulted for the cost of an extra two credits, but such entries are only available online for records not bound by the respective closure periods for births, marriages or deaths. The RCE cannot be searched as an independent database in its own right.

A guide for all the statutory registers within this collection can be found at **www.scotlandspeople.gov.uk/guides/statutory-registers**.

*ii) Church Registers*

Prior to 1855, the key records noting vital information are the surviving parish registers of the established Church of Scotland ('the Kirk'), the Roman Catholic Church, and the various dissenting Presbyterian denominations.

The history of the Kirk in Scotland prior to 1855 is somewhat turbulent, but can be summarised as follows. The Reformation of 1560 replaced the Roman Catholic system of church governance with a new Presbyterian structure, but for the next 130 years factions of the Kirk fought with the Crown over the issue of control. Following the Union of the Crowns in 1603, the Crown wished to bring Scotland into line with English practice, through an episcopal form of governance, i.e. with bishops in charge. The Presbyterians had other ideas and eventually won through at the 'Glorious Revolution' of 1689, but a faction split off to form what was to become the Scottish Episcopal Church.

The Presbyterians' victory was dented when owners of land on which parish churches were located secured the right of 'patronage' in 1712, to allow them to decide who the minister of a congregation should be, rather than the congregations concerned. This led to internal divisions between those who would play ball, and those who opposed the Act, followed by a series of schisms in 1740 (the Original Secession and the Associate Synod), 1763 (the Relief Church) and 1843 (the Free Church of Scotland). Some of these split further, while various factions later united to form the United Secession and the United Presbyterian churches. In the meantime, the Irish Famine from 1845–51 saw a significant influx of Irish refugees arriving; this led to a massive revival in the Roman Catholic Church, which had not quite disappeared at the Reformation, surviving in parts of the Highlands and Islands.

The result of all of this is that ScotlandsPeople hosts a significant amount of church records for three separate groupings:

*Church of Scotland* – the Kirk's parish records, known as the 'Old Parish Registers' or 'OPRs', date back to 1553 for the parish of Errol in Perthshire, just seven years before the Reformation. Their surviving coverage varies dramatically for parishes across the country, with many registers not existing prior to the eighteenth or even nineteenth century in parts. To understand what is available, visit the NRS's 'Coverage of the Old Parish Registers' page at **www.nrscotland.gov.uk/research/guides/old-parish-registers/list-of-old-parish-registers**. The cut-off point on ScotlandsPeople is the year 1855, when civil registration records take over.

*Roman Catholic Church* – the Catholic Parish Registers ('CPRs') include the surviving records of many, but not all, Roman Catholic congregations in Scotland, with the majority from the 1840s onwards. In addition to records sourced from the Scottish Catholic Archives, material is also included from the Bishopric of the Forces collection as held in Aldershot, England. Records go beyond 1855, with a listing of available congregations at **www. scotlandspeople.gov.uk/guides/church-registers**. Note that FindmyPast has a much larger Scottish Roman Catholic records collection available – see p.49.

*Other churches* – it is important to note that this category holds records from Presbyterian dissenting denominations alone, and only those that later reunited with the main Kirk; several Presbyterian denominations remain separate to the Kirk to this day. A guide to what is included is available at **www.scotlandspeople.gov.uk/guides/church-registers**. There are no records within this collection for other denominations, such as the Scottish Episcopal Church, Methodists or Jews.

The records are accessible through four separate search screens, and you need to tick the box for the relevant record grouping (i.e. Church of Scotland, Roman Catholic Church or Other churches). The cost to view any entry found is six credits.

*Births and baptisms* – an initial search for a birth or baptism allows you to type in the name and surname of a child, the gender, year range, county and parish/congregation. When the results are returned, you will then see the surname, forename, parents'/other details, gender, date, parish number, reference number and name of the parish, and button allowing you to view the original. These results can be reordered by clicking on the headers, for example to allow you to see the parents displayed in alphabetical order (by the father's first name), or in chronological order.

Once the results are returned, you can also further filter them by using search boxes to the left of the screen. You will find two new search boxes here marked '1st Parent Name' and '2nd Parent Name', which can allow you to do a parental search, typing in the names of parents only to find a list of baptised children noted for them. (A similar facility is available through the FamilySearch website for OPR indexes – see p.47.)

Three key points to bear in mind with baptismal searches are:

• A child's name may not always be recorded (e.g. 'on this day, John McDonald had a lawful daughter baptised'), so leaving the child's forename field blank in a search may be worth trying if nothing is immediately found.

- The mother's name may also not be noted (as shown previously), meaning that a search which includes her name may fail to locate the child; in such a case, try removing her name in the 2nd Parent Name field and repeat the search.
- The mother will always be noted with her maiden name in Scottish parish records; under Scots Law, she never lost it after marriage.

*Banns and marriages* – banns were required to be proclaimed three times on successive Sundays for a forthcoming marriage. You may find a record of all three occurrences, or simply the first calling of the banns – in some cases, you might only find a record of the payment of money from the kirk sessions for the banns to be proclaimed. Unless the record states the date of marriage, the calling of the banns is in itself not proof that the marriage actually happened, only that it was intended.

Banns could be called in two separate parishes for the intending spouses, but this does not mean that two marriages occurred! In such instances, it was traditional for a marriage to take place in the bride's parish, which may or may not be noted. Irregular marriage (p.33) was also perfectly valid in Scotland, and as such, no church-based record may exist; in such circumstances, a disciplinary record might be available within the kirk session records.

It is also worth knowing that prior to 1834, Dissenting and Nonconformist churches could not legally carry out marriages, with the exception of the Scottish Episcopal Church (from 1711). If they did, such marriages were considered as irregular marriages, with the minister being the witness and not the celebrant. From 1834 this changed when such bodies could perform marriages so long as the banns were first proclaimed by the Church of Scotland parish church. This means that banns records noted by a parish church in the OPRs from 1834–1855 may not necessarily be for marriages that took place within that church.

*Deaths and burials* – the coverage of burial registers for parishes across Scotland is incredibly poor. In some cases, the records are not for burials at all, but for the hire of mortcloths as noted in the kirk session minutes or accounts, which were used to drape over the coffin. The churches were not the only body offering to hire out a mortcloth, with trade incorporations in the royal burghs, for example, offering their own trade cloths.

It is also worth noting that women can also be poorly described in such records, for example as 'Widow MacFarlane', and so it may not be easy to confirm that you have the right candidate.

*Other events* – although this screen contains tick boxes for both the 'Roman Catholic Church' and 'Other Events', the overwhelming majority of records in this dataset are from the Catholic Church (the rest being records from two United Presbyterian congregations in Dunbar and Dalkeith).

The Catholic records available are sourced from various collections, with each search return providing the name and an 'event code' letter beside them. They include the following categories, with the event code in brackets:

- Communicants and Converts (U & I) – these note lists of parishioners.
- Confessions (E) – not the records of confession (!), but of attendance.
- Confirmation (event code I) – a childhood sacrament undertaken before the teen years, which may note the child's confirmation name (a saint's name).
- Converts (V) – normally noting conversions from other faiths taken during adulthood.
- Seat Rents (R) – noting those who paid a fee for a particular pew in the parish church.
- Sick calls (S) – noting visitations by priests to sick parishioners.
- *Status Animarum* (A) – a form of church census literally meaning 'state of the souls'; in some cases providing details of age and even date of birth.

### iii) Census returns

A decennial census has been recorded in Britain from 1801, though the 1841 census was the first to be genealogically useful in listing names of those present in each household on census night. Each census offers additional details on where individuals were born, their ages, and their occupation, effectively providing a snapshot of life once every ten years. Importantly, from 1851 onwards the records also note the relationship of everybody within a property to the 'head of household', making them important documentary tools for reconstituting historic family groupings. A guide to the records, and the information that can be found within them, is available at **www.scotlandspeople.gov.uk/guides/census-returns**.

While other platforms offer census transcriptions online (p.57), ScotlandsPeople is the only website to offer images of census records from 1841–1901, with the site also offering exclusive access to the 1911 census. Unlike the rest of Britain and Ireland, the original household schedules for the 1911 Scottish census have not survived, with the

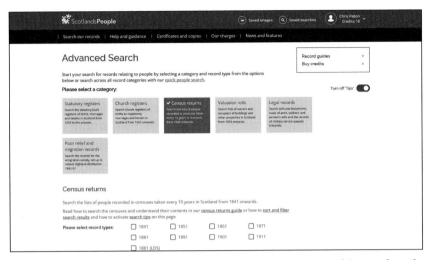

*ScotlandsPeople is the only online platform where you can see original images from the 1841–1911 censuses.*

information instead presented via two-page-long enumerators' returns, the information having been transcribed from the original schedules before they were destroyed. The 1921 census, which is closed to access for 100 years, will also be made available on the platform in 2021.

At the start of the main census search page you will be asked to tick the census of interest, with boxes available from 1841 to 1911. Fields are then provided for a surname, forename, forename of another person on that census page, gender, age range, and county and district (Scottish registration districts largely mirror the parishes and registration districts as used in civil registration). If an entry is found, the index entry returned will include surname, forename, year, gender, age at census, a reference number for the registration district and name of that district, along with the county, and a button to provide access. The cost to access most census images is six credits, but in some cases an entry may start at the bottom of one page and conclude on the following, for which you will need to pay to view each page.

There are two options available for the 1881 census, with the box marked '1881 (LDS)' providing free access to transcribed entries from this census as transcribed by the Church of Jesus Christ of Latter Day Saints. The field names offered here are slightly different, with some advantages and disadvantages. Searches can be carried out by surname, forename, gender and age range, but there is no option to search with the name of a second person in the household. Rather than offering county and district fields, 'address' and 'census place' fields are offered instead, along with an incredibly useful field for 'birth place'.

If an entry is found in this collection for 1881, the index information returned is the surname, forename, year, gender, age, an LDS reference number, the address, census place (including district/parish and county) and the birth place (including district/parish and county). The final button is marked 'View image (free)'; clicking on this does not take you to the census record image, but a transcript of the record for the whole household, with additional source information noted at the top of the entry; this can be downloaded as a free PDF document.

### iv) Valuation rolls

Valuation rolls were records to assist with taxation which noted the rental value, notional or actual, of a property. From 1855 the records were compiled annually by 15 August in the counties and within the royal and parliamentary burghs, with the process continuing until 1989. A detailed guide on the collection is available at **www.scotlandspeople. gov.uk/guides/valuation-rolls**.

Although most of the valuation rolls have been digitised by the NRS, they have been indexed only for every tenth year at the mid-census intervals, i.e. 1855–56, 1865–66, etc up to 1915–16, and then for every fifth year up to 1955–56. On ScotlandsPeople, at the time of writing the rolls that have been made available are for the years 1855, 1865, 1875, 1885, 1895, 1905, 1915, 1920, 1925, 1930, 1935 and 1940, though this may extend further in due course. Between the census years, and beyond 1911, they can act as a useful census substitute in noting whether a member of a family (usually but not always the head of the household) was still based at a known location, or whether he or she had moved.

The search screen allows you to search by surname, forename, group (e.g. a business, trust, or public authority), status ('tenants and occupiers' or 'owners'), county/city, parish, burgh/city, and place (acting as a keyword search option, although you cannot use numbers for street addresses with this). The returned index entry will freely offer these details, along with the VR reference number, and a button allowing you to view the original image, at a cost of two credits. The original image itself may offer additional information, such as the name of the proprietor (feudal superior or landlord), the tenant or occupier, a description of the holding, the rateable value, and the rent or feu duty payable.

### v) Legal records

This section of ScotlandsPeople contains four categories of records which were derived from court-based processes or tribunals. A detailed guide providing an overview of the records is available at **www. scotlandspeople.gov.uk/guides/legal-records**.

*Wills and testaments* – although initially handled by ecclesiastical courts in the medieval period, from 1562 until the present day Scotland's confirmation process (the equivalent of 'probate' in the rest of the UK), has been handled by the country's civil courts, initially through the commissary courts, and then from the 1830s onwards the Sheriff Courts.

If a person died after leaving a will, they were said to be 'testate'. After an inventory was compiled of the deceased's movable estate (e.g. money, possessions, but not property or land) and any money owed or owing, the court would empower an executor to administer the estate as per the instructions in the will. In such cases, the resulting document generated by the court was called a 'testament testamentar'. If, however, the deceased was 'intestate', with no will left behind, then the court would appoint an executor to administer the estate through a document called a 'testament dative'.

Unlike the rest of the UK, land could not be bequeathed in a Scottish will until 1868, although prior to this it was possible to put your property into a trust to be administered while alive, with an indication of how you wished for it to be managed following death. In such cases a 'trust disposition and settlement' is another document to look out for.

ScotlandsPeople has digitised all surviving testaments dating back to 1513 and made them available online up to 1925. The index allows users to look for such documents by surname, forename, year range, description (title, occupation or place), and the court or commissariot (the jurisdiction of a commissary court). The cost of a document is ten credits, irrespective of how many pages it is comprised of.

Further online records concerning Scottish inheritance are discussed on p.54.

*Soldiers' and airmen's wills* – in addition to domestic confirmation documents, ScotlandsPeople offers wills from 26,000 soldiers and airmen, as recorded from 1857–1965. The majority of records are from the First World War, but there are also wills left by military personnel serving in the South African War, the Second World War and the Korean War.

Records can be searched by surname, forename, year of death, service number, rank, regiment and place of death. The cost of a document is ten credits, irrespective of the number of pages.

Additional military wills resources are discussed on p.95, while service records and other military documentation are discussed in Chapter 4.

*Military service appeals tribunal* – this database contains Military Tribunal documents from 1916–1918 for those seeking exemption from conscription into the UK armed forces. Most records were destroyed after the war, with the only surviving documents from Scotland being those from tribunals held in Armadale, Bathgate, Blackridge, Bo'ness, Bonnyrigg, Broxburn, the Central Appeal Tribunal, Cockenzie, Cockenzie Port Seton burgh, Dalkeith, East Linton, East Lothian, Edinburgh, Dundee, Glasgow (just two cases), Haddington, Innerleithen, Lasswade, Leith, Lewis, Linlithgow, Loanhead, Midlothian, North Berwick, Paisley, Peebles, Penicuik, Prestonpans, South Queensferry, Stornoway, Tranent, Uphall, West Lothian and Whitburn.

Records can be searched by surname, forename, year, age, occupation, address, grounds of appeal, tribunal, appeal number, and notes (including places, relatives, or business names). The documents cost twenty credits each, irrespective of the number of pages contained.

*Coats of arms* – this database provides access to two volumes of the *Public Register of All Arms and Bearings* from 1672–1916, as kept by the Court of the Lord Lyon in Edinburgh, Scotland's heraldic authority.

In Scotland, arms can be granted to a person only if they are deemed by the Lord Lyon King of Arms to be 'virtuous and well deserving', and come within his jurisdiction. Anybody born or resident within Scotland, and within parts of the British Commonwealth, can apply for a 'Grant of Arms'. (For those living in England, Wales or Ireland, applications for such grants must be made to their own respective heraldic authorities.) A person's coat of arms belongs to one individual or body only, and cannot be legally used in Scotland unless included within the public register. Arms are also considered to be heritable property (i.e. they can be inherited), while the illegal use of arms can be prosecuted by the court, which has its own procurator fiscal (public prosecutor).

The entries from the first volume of the register from 1672–1804 are quite brief, providing in most cases just a written description of a person's arms, known as a 'blazon', although some are illustrated. From 1804, blazons in the second volume are accompanied by hand-painted depictions of the arms granted, and a brief summary of the genealogies of the petitioners, if recorded when the application was made. This may go back a mere generation or two, or considerably further if an ancestor was also 'armigerous' (entitled to bear arms).

The register can be searched by name and year range only. The cost per document download is a hefty forty credits.

*vi) Poor relief and migration records*
At the time of writing this is a relatively new category, hosting one record set:

*Highlands and Islands emigration* – this is a database which has also been previously hosted in an index-based form on the SCAN website (p.44), and which contains passenger records from the Highlands and Islands Emigration Society from 1852–1857, detailing 4,919 people who were assisted by the body with passage to Australia from the west of Scotland. The background to the collection is explored at **www.scotlandspeople. gov.uk/guides/highland-and-island-emigration-society-records**.

Records can be searched by surname, forename, ship name, arrival port, and the county/city of origin in Scotland, being Argyll, Caithness, Inverness, Ross and Cromarty, and Midlothian. After an initial search, the results can be further refined by filters to the left of the search page for a passenger's departure port, residence and parish in Scotland.

This particular collection is completely free to access.

## Search for Places
The 'Search for Places' menu option of the Search Our Records page in fact leads to one of the site's many detailed guide pages (p.44), but also hosts some valuable research advice and resources that can help you to search for people by place.

*Maps and Plans* – this screen permits you to locate more than 2,400 historic maps, plans and drawings from the NRS's Register House Plans, as drawn from a substantially larger collection of more than 170,000 documents held at the archive's Thomas Thomson House facility. A dedicated guide to the collection is available at **www.scotlandspeople. gov.uk/guides/maps-and-plans**.

The collection can be searched by typing a place name into the 'Search for' box, or by typing an NRS catalogue number (p.5) for a particular plan if known, which will be prefixed with 'RHP'. You can also search by year range, county and parish. All returned maps and plans documents are free to view, and have been digitised to a very high resolution, which means that you can really zoom in to view some superb detail, particularly for documents such as architectural plans.

*Searching indexed records by place* – this section of the page offers tips on how to search by place within the collections previously detailed in the 'Search for People' records section of the site.

*County guides* – this offers a series of pages for each county within Scotland, explaining the administrative boundaries found within them. The most interesting part of each county guide is the section providing information on which commissary courts and sheriff courts were utilised by people from that county, with the relevant NRS catalogue numbers for the collections.

## Image Library

ScotlandsPeople's Image Library allows users to view over 2,000 photographs and document images sourced from the NRS. A series of categories are listed on the left of the screen, ranging from 'Aerial Photography' to 'World Cultures', and you can also search by keyword, reference number and time period.

If a copy of a record is sought, it can be purchased for £15 plus VAT. As the records are Crown copyright, they can be used for a variety of purposes, including publications and broadcasts. The platform has an Image Licensing page at **www.scotlandspeople.gov.uk/image-licensing** with further details.

## Other Main Menu Options

From the home page main menu there are several other options that can assist with research and additional services.

### i) Help and Guidance

This menu item offers a gateway to six different areas of the site:

*Guidance about records and research* – this section can be considered the encyclopaedia area on ScotlandsPeople, with various pages grouped under three headings, Record Guides, Topics, and How to Research. The main page offers a 'Search our guides for advice' box, which allows you to perform searches for words and phrases across all the contents.

The Record Guides listing offers links to all the help pages specifically describing the content found within the records collections on ScotlandsPeople. There is a Record Guides A–Z, followed by dedicated links to introductory platforms for Statutory Registers, Church Registers and Census Returns.

The Topics list includes a link to Topics A–Z page, offering pages on useful information such as the registration of illegitimate births, emigration and immigration, and an exploration of unfamiliar words and phrases. This list is then followed by links to three topics: Agricultural produce and livestock, Counties, cities and burghs, and Dates, numbers and sums of money – essentially the first three topics from the main A–Z list.

The How to Research list offers a How to Research A–Z, covering topics such as Family History, House and Building History, Photographic and Image Research, and Social History.

*Technical issues* – this section has many useful areas, including a list of items that the ScotlandsPeople team is currently working on, information on accessibility to the site if disabled, details on how to change password, advice on printing out records, some search tips, how to change viewer functions, and how to use the Timelines function.

*Frequently Asked Questions* – information on charges, copyright, a very basic general section, information on which records are available (and on future records), and the use of vouchers on the site.

*Explore the site* – a broad overview on what to expect from the site for newcomers, with links to topic guides available throughout the platform.

*What records are in the site* – this page is worth bookmarking, as it provides quick links to some of the most useful pages about background information on various records categories.

The page provides access to five categories of records: Statutory registers, Census returns, Church registers, Valuation rolls, Legal records,

*ScotlandsPeople's research guides provide an overview of what is available on the site, and, just as importantly, what is not.*

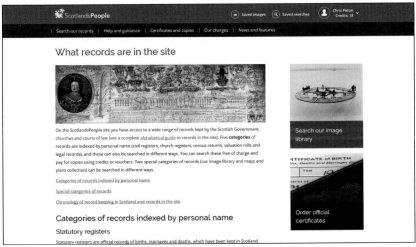

as well as special categories, such as Photographs and illustrations, and Maps and plans.

Of particular interest is a 'Chronology of record keeping in Scotland and records in the site', from 1127, when the earliest royal charter as held at the NRS was recorded, to 2014, when the registration of same-sex marriages commenced.

*Visit us* – this provides information for those planning a visit to the ScotlandsPeople Centre in Edinburgh, as well as links to family history centres in other parts of the country.

### ii) Certificates and Copies

For family history purposes, digital copies of records are more than enough to provide the information needed to establish relationships and details on people's lives. However, when applying for a passport or driving license, or for certain employment needs, a certified copy of an original may be required.

This section of ScotlandsPeople provides detailed guides on how to apply for such records, methods for ordering both online and by other means, and information on the costs incurred, as presented on the Our Charges page (below).

### iii) Our Charges

This page provides a brief overview of costs incurred in using ScotlandsPeople records, including how to purchase pay-per-view images (with a link to buy credits), costs for official extracts, and a link to redeem ScotlandsPeople vouchers, which can be purchased at many libraries and institutions across the country (and at a discount).

The final part of the page also lists the costs for visiting the ScotlandsPeople Centre, and a link to make an online booking for such a trip.

### iv) News and Features

This final section essentially offers an online blog with news updates and occasional articles, often tied in with new records releases. The contents can be searched by keyword.

*Chapter 3*

# WHO WERE THEY? FURTHER SOURCES

While ScotlandsPeople is by far the most important and comprehensive platform for primary records, there are many websites offering alternative presentations of the resources on the site, as well as other unique offerings. In this chapter I will explore additional resources that can help identify who our ancestors once were, and how they lived their lives.

## Further Scottish vital records

FamilySearch (p.22) has previously photographed some of the Scottish civil registration records at the NRS for the period from 1855–1875, 1881 and 1891, but for births and marriages only. It offers free to access indexes for these online, included within three collections:

- Scotland Births and Baptisms, 1564–1950
  **www.familysearch.org/search/collection/1771030**
- Scotland Marriages, 1561–1910
  **www.familysearch.org/search/collection/1771074**
- International Genealogical Index (IGI)
  **www.familysearch.org/search/collection/igi**

Note that the IGI, an earlier FamilySearch database with worldwide vital records holdings, essentially carries the same Scottish coverage for civil registration records as the previous two collections. It is important to note that the IGI is split into two separate parts, the 'Community Contributed IGI' and the 'Community Indexed IGI'. The 'contributed' records in the first part are unverified patron submissions from members of the LDS

*FamilySearch's birth records index includes statutory records from 1855–1875, as well as Church of Scotland and dissenter Presbyterian church records.*

church, whereas the 'indexed' records are those formally extracted from primary sources.

When searching for births, the information returned in the databases will be the name of the child, the date of birth, the district of registration, and the names of both parents or the mother (if illegitimate). With marriages, you will find the names of both spouses, the date of marriage and the district of registration. In all cases, FamilySearch will also provide citation information from its own microfilmed collections.

The digitised images for these records, as well as death records for the same years, can be accessed at FamilySearch's network of family history centres, or affiliate centres. The catalogue page hosting these collections can be found at **www.familysearch.org/search/catalog/79310?availability=Family%20History%20Library**, where you will notice a symbol of a camera with a key above it, signifying restricted access.

The year ranges of the first two collections noted are clearly wider than the civil records collections described. This is because the datasets also include indexed entries for church records, the majority being Church of Scotland registers from prior to 1855, but also additional records from some dissenting parishes before and after 1855. The records are sourced from both the IGI and a successor project called the British Isles Vital Records Index (BVRI). A useful guide to understand what is contained in the IGI for each county is Steve Archer's website at **www.archersoftware.co.uk/igi/fs-sct.htm**; a list of Scottish records gathered through the BVRI can be identified at **https://bit.ly/BVRI**. If a parish name is listed with no denomination, then this will be for a Church of Scotland parish church. Those sourced from other churches will state the denomination after the parish name. Note that these databases are also freely available on Ancestry, FindmyPast and MyHeritage (see p.24).

For the most recent decades Ancestry offers a database entitled 'Scotland and Northern Ireland, Death Index, 1989–2018', located at **www.ancestry.co.uk/search/collections/scotniredeathidx**. The records are sourced from 'GreyPower Deceased Data, compiled by Wilmington Millennium, West Yorkshire', with the page further noting that 'this collection is a compiled index that covers approximately 45% of the total deaths that occurred in this time period', although it does not indicate how this proportion applies to both countries. The database provides the deceased's name, sex, date of birth or age at death, date of death, and residence at time of death, but no source information to tie in with the death registrations. Some records for the Crown dependencies of Jersey and the Isle of Man are also included.

In some cases, death was not the final act involving our ancestors. Available on Old Scottish at **www.oldscottish.com/anatomy-registers. html** are records from anatomy registers from 1842–1949, detailing the names of people whose bodies were dissected by anatomists and medical students in the name of science (as sourced from NRS series MH1). The records including registers from Aberdeen, Dundee, Glasgow, Edinburgh, and St Andrews.

FamilySearch offers a database entitled 'Scotland Presbyterian & Protestant Church Records, 1736–1990', with dissenting Presbyterian church records from the NRS's CH3 series, comprised of holdings for the Free Church, United Presbyterian, United Free and other Protestant churches, available at **www.familysearch.org/search/collection/2421466**. Original images from these records can be viewed by LDS members, at a FamilySearch family history centre, or at affiliate centres.

Ancestry has further holdings within its 'Scotland, Extracted Parish Records, 1571–1997' (**www.ancestry.co.uk/search/collections/ scotlandextpar/**), as obtained from various published resources, while indexes to additional church records can be found on Scottish Indexes and Old Scottish.

FindmyPast has four collections for Roman Catholic ancestry, which, as with the CPRs on ScotlandsPeople (p.36), are sourced from the Scottish Catholic Archives. The collections are:

- Scotland Roman Catholic Parish Baptisms
- Scotland Roman Catholic Parish Marriages
- Scotland Roman Catholic Parish Burials
- Scotland Roman Catholic Parish Congregational Records

The last of these contains registers of confirmations and communions, parish lists, seat rentals, and lists of converts to Catholicism across Scotland. At the time of writing the source information notes that there are no records for Shetland, Berwickshire, Kinross or Clackmannanshire.

The FreeREG website at **www.freereg.org.uk** has indexes to a small number of dissenting and nonconformist Scottish parish records, while the Internet Archive is further worth searching for some published holdings. FindmyPast has two further collections to help plug the gaps. The 'Scotland, Antenuptial Relationship Index 1661–1780' collection sources instances of kirk session discipline for those who conceived an illegitimate child prior to marriage, while the 'Scotland, Irregular & Cross-Border Marriage Index' dataset flags up marriages for those who availed themselves of Scots Law to marry irregularly once across the border from England.

For Jewish research in Scotland visit the Scottish Jewish Archives Centre at **www.sjac.org.uk**, and the JewishGen and JGSGB UK database at **www.jewishgen.org/databases/UK**. The Knowles Collection database for the British Isles is another useful research tool, now located on FamilySearch within its 'Genealogies' section. Type in the name and search terms of interest, and select 'Community Trees' in the menu box at the bottom of the page just before the 'Search' button. The results are presented in a family tree display.

## Other UK vital records

Your Scottish ancestors may have relocated to other parts of the UK at some stage in their lives, or indeed may have been born outside of Scotland in the UK before moving to the country. The civil registration systems in England, Wales and Ireland are completely separate to those in Scotland, but the records they generated can equally help.

Registration commenced in England and Wales in July 1837. Although the period for which records are available is almost two decades longer, the information returned is not as detailed as found within Scottish records. In English and Welsh birth records, for example, the time of birth is only noted for multiple births, such as twins and triplets, and no date of marriage is noted. In marriage records, only the spouses' fathers are named, and not their mothers, while for death records there is no information on parents at all, unless the informant was a parent (such as in the case of infant deaths). Another major difference is that unlike Scotland, where irregular marriage did not end until 1940, it did so in England and Wales almost two centuries earlier in 1754.

Records for England and Wales were compiled by local superintendent registrars in quarterly returns consistently from 1837–1983, and thereafter on an annual basis, and sent to the English-based General Register Office (GRO). Several websites host the indexes up to 2006. FreeBMD at **www. freebmd.org.uk** is a volunteer project offering transcribed indexes online for free; for the nineteenth century the database is virtually complete, while a significant amount of records for the twentieth century are already uploaded. Several commercial vendors also provide access, including Ancestry, FindmyPast The Genealogist, MyHeritage, and FamilyRelatives. Once you have found the correct index reference number you can order a copy of the required record from the GRO in Southport, via **www.gro.gov.uk/gro/content/certificates/default.asp**.

In Ireland, civil registration started in two phases, with the information returned in records broadly at the same level as that for England and Wales, all overseen by the GRO for Ireland in Dublin. The registration of non-Roman Catholic marriages (essentially Protestant denominations and civil marriages, which could involve Roman Catholics) commenced in April 1845, but it was not until January 1864 that births, deaths and marriage registration for all denominations and none took place. A further development was the establishment of a separate GRO in Belfast for Northern Ireland after the Partition of Ireland in 1921, with the GRO in Dublin continuing to administer to the counties which became the Irish Free State and later the Republic of Ireland.

Irish civil registration records can be obtained from two websites, at the free **www.irishgenealogy.ie** for the Republic and at the pay-per-view

*The author's grandmother Jean Paton, née Currie, was born in Bridgeton, Glasgow, in 1904 but died in Carrickfergus, Northern Ireland, in 1979.*

**https://geni.nidirect.gov.uk** for Northern Ireland. Both sites offer records for Northern Ireland prior to 1922, but as with ScotlandsPeople, they each respect closure periods for privacy, of 100 years for births, 75 years for marriages and 50 years for deaths. Unlike ScotlandsPeople, however, there are no indexes online for these closed periods. GRO indexes for Irish records are available from 1845–1958 on FamilySearch, Ancestry and FindmyPast (covering events for Northern Ireland only up to 1921), which can help with the location of more recent birth and marriage events.

Additional civil records held by the GRO in England are those for British events registered overseas. There are several such collections, including military chaplaincy services (1796–1880), regimental birth registers (1761–1924), Army Returns and Service Department Registrations (1880–1965), consular and High Commission services, registers of shipping and seamen, and much more. Many records for Scotland are included in the relevant BMD databases on ScotlandsPeople (in the 'Minor Records' category within each database), but not all; for example, the army chaplaincy records which go back to the 1760s. To order such an overseas certificate online you need to register with the English GRO website at **www.gro.gov.uk/gro/content/certificates/default.asp**. Once logged in, click on 'Order a Certificate / PDF' to access the application page. Then select the option you need within the section headed 'For overseas events which were registered with the British authorities', and place your order. Additional overseas records can be found on BMD Registers (p.21), as well as Ancestry, FindmyPast and TheGenealogist.

For English and Welsh parish records prior to the start of registration, Ancestry, FindmyPast and TheGenealogist have an extensive range of records available. For Ireland, Roman Catholic parish registers prior to 1880 are freely available to browse at Registers NLI (**https://registers.nli.ie**), with third party indexes for this collection also freely available on Ancestry and FindmyPast. The subscription based RootsIreland (**www.rootsireland.ie**) provides access to transcripts from registers of many denominations across the island.

## Burials

Following on from death records are records for burials, which can exist in two forms: the records of interment or cremation, and the wording that may be found on gravestone inscriptions, often referred to in Scotland as 'monumental inscriptions'.

For records of burials, the best resource online is that for the city of Glasgow, with many burial and lair registers freely available to view through the FamilySearch catalogue at **https://bit.ly/GlasgowCemeteryRecords**. The pay-per-view site DeceasedOnline (p.23) has additional records available for Aberdeen City and Aberdeenshire, and Edinburgh Crematorium.

SAFHS hosts a database at **www.safhs.org.uk/burialgrounds.php** noting the details of over 3,500 burial grounds across Scotland. The database can be searched by county, parish or by keyword search. If a burial ground is noted, the following information will be provided about it: parish, county, alternative name, whether it still exists, OS grid reference, latitude and longitude, the local authority responsible for it, the type of burial ground, denomination, memorials, whether surveyed, dates opened and closed (and 'ancient burials'), where known OPR and kirk session records may be held, if pre-1855 monumental inscriptions have been recorded, if later memorials have been recorded, whether published, and where such monumental inscription information can be found. Finally, the database also advises if a ground is included in the National Burial Index and the National Monument Register of Scotland, along with any additional notes of worth.

There are several online resources hosting gravestone inscriptions. A team from Scottish Monumental Inscriptions (**www.scottish-monumental-inscriptions.com**) regularly tours around the country to photograph and transcribe headstones, with the records available to purchase on CD, or by download from the site (many of the team's records can also be accessed from FindmyPast and the Deceased Online website).

FindaGrave (**www.findagrave.com**) and BillionGraves (**www.billiongraves.com**) are volunteer-based sites with coverage from around the world, including Scotland, with many entries including photographs of the relevant headstones; FamilySearch also provides access to both databases through its Scotland page. FindaGrave's entries can be searched on Ancestry via its 'UK and Ireland, Find A Grave Index, 1300s–Current' database, while FindmyPast provides access to BillionGraves through its 'Scotland Billion Graves Cemetery Index' collection, and MyHeritage through its 'BillionGraves' section. Some previously published burial records, such as interments from Aberdeenshire and Edinburgh, can be found also on Ancestry, within its 'Scotland, Extracted Parish Records, 1571–1997' collection (p.49).

Highland Memorial Inscriptions (**https://sites.google.com/site/highland memorialinscriptions/home**) notes burials from much of the Highlands, including major cemeteries such as Tomnahurich in Inverness, while Memento Mori (**www.memento-mori.co.uk**) has also indexed records from Glasgow and much of the Central Belt. The Friends of Dundee City Archives (**www.fdca.org.uk**) hosts several burial collections including one for Dundee's Howff Cemetery and another for Broughty Ferry. Additional sites providing access to transcriptions and/or photographs of gravestone inscriptions include Interment.net (**www.interment.net/uk/scot/index. htm**), Gravestone Photos (**www.gravestonephotos.com**), and Find a Grave in Scotland (**www.findagraveinscotland.com**).

Finally, many Scots also died in times of war. The Commonwealth War Graves Commission website at **www.cwgc.org** records the known burials of, or places of commemoration for, soldiers killed in both world wars. In addition, original records describing the interment process are also now available for many of those commemorated on the site, noting inscriptions to be added to headstones, and the next of kin with whom the Commission was liaising at the time. Photographs of many of the memorials in Scotland commemorating their sacrifice have been photographed by the Scottish Military Research Group, and can be freely accessed at **www.scottishmilitaryresearch.co.uk**.

## Confirmation and probate records

ScotlandsPeople hosts the various wills and testamentary records that were granted through the confirmation process (p.41). Another source that can help to determine where the assets of a deceased Scot went to is the annual *Calendars of Confirmations and Inventories*, which provides short abridgements of the testaments granted, noting the name of the deceased, date and place of death, the value of the estate and details of any executors appointed. These exist from 1876 to 1959, although can only be found online up to 1936 via Ancestry's 'Scotland, National Probate Index (Calendar of Confirmations and Inventories), 1876–1936' collection.

Scotland differs from the rest of the UK in that historically there have been very separate procedures in place for the inheritance of different types of estate. From 1868 onwards wills found on ScotlandsPeople can note both the 'moveable' estate (such as money and household items) and 'heritable' estate (land and property) left by an individual. Prior to 1868, however, land and property could not be bequeathed in a Scottish will.

In order to inherit heritable estate, a prospective heir, usually the eldest son or next in line as per the rules of primogeniture, had to be formally recognised first as the 'apparent heir' by the deceased's feudal superior, from whom the land was held. This could be done in two ways. If the land was held directly from the Crown, then the heir had to go through a jury-based process called the Services of Heirs. If the land was instead held from someone who was a 'subject superior' (i.e. someone else who was a subject of the Crown), then all he or she needed was a document called a 'precept of clare constat' to be granted from the subject superior, which essentially notes that it is clearly understood that the apparent heir was who he or she said they were.

For those who went through the Services of Heirs process, a series of abridgements are freely available online which can tell you when the judgement by the jury was returned or 'retoured' to the Scottish Chancery, with such returns noted as 'services' or 'retours'. There were in fact two types of retours: those simply confirming the identity of the apparent heir (known as a 'general service' or a 'general retour'), and those completing the inheritance process, vesting the apparent heir after recognition in the possession of the lands and properties in question (known as a 'special service' or a 'special retour'), and including details of such property, including its 'extent' or value.

For the period from 1700–1859 the Services of Heirs indexes can be found through the FamilySearch catalogue at **www.familysearch.org/search/catalog/1004156**. The records are presented in a series of browse-only decennial indexes (in ten-year runs) on a single digital microfilm, in alphabetical order. Each entry notes the name of the heir who was served by the jury, 'distinguishing particulars' which give details of the deceased and the heir's relationship to the deceased, as well as the date of the judgement, followed by the date of recording and index information for the full volumes. The original records are held at the NRS, but the indexes usually provide enough genealogical information to establish relationships.

*The Services of Heirs indexes, which note the heirs of heritable estate, are available to browse on FamilySearch through its catalogue.*

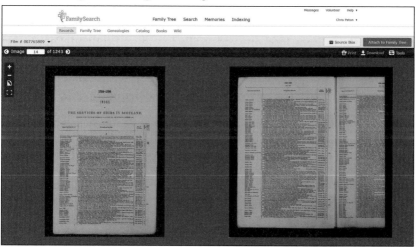

Prior to 1700 it gets a bit more complicated, with the indexes compiled in a slightly different way and, just for fun, in Latin – although it is usually easy enough to work out the basics of what is going on. The records from 1544–1699 are presented in three volumes of the *Inquisitionum ad Capellam Domini Regis Retornatarum quae in Publicis Archivis Scotiae adhuc Servantur, Abbreviatio*. These can be found on FamilySearch at **www.familysearch.org/search/catalog/248869**, and also on GoogleBooks at **https://bit.ly/retours1** (Volume 1), **https://bit.ly/retours2** (Volume 2) and **https://bit.ly/retours3** (Volume 3).

Volumes 1 and 2 cover the special services, with Volume 2 also holding abridgements to general services. Indexes for both are found in Volume 3, which also holds indexes for appointments of tutors to those inheriting in their minority ('brieves of tutory'), or those not sound of mind ('brieves of idiotry' or 'of furiosity'), together forming the *Inquisitiones de Tutela*. Further information on the Services of Heirs and the weird and wonderful world of Scottish inheritance can be found in my book *Tracing Your Scottish Ancestry Through Church and State Records* (see Appendix).

If your Scottish ancestor died elsewhere in Britain, it is still worth checking the ScotlandsPeople wills collection. A record from an English, Welsh or Irish court (or indeed any overseas courts) confirming executry may well have been 'resealed' by the Scottish courts, if the deceased had estate in Scotland as well as in his or her new abode. The confirmation process outside of Scotland is usually referred to as 'probate', and prior to 1858 was handled by the ecclesiastical courts of the Anglican Church, becoming a civil process thereafter. The equivalent of a testament testamentar (p.9) in these courts is known as a 'grant of probate', while a testament dative is paralleled by 'letters of administration' or 'admons'.

From 1858 onwards, a series of free-to-search calendars is available through Ancestry's 'England & Wales, National Probate Calendar (Index of Wills and Administrations), 1858–1995', and also at the UK Government's Find a Will site at **https://probatesearch.service.gov.uk**, from where copies of the original wills can also be ordered. A third source for the calendars is FamilySearch's 'England and Wales, National Index of Wills and Administrations, 1858–1957' collection, the benefit with this version being that you can also search for the names of those who may have been beneficiaries.

Earlier records from English and Welsh ecclesiastical courts can be found on Ancestry, FindmyPast and TheGenealogist. Northern Irish wills records from 1858–1965 can be found on the PRONI website at

**www.nidirect.gov.uk/proni**, with additional Irish wills for the Republic and earlier periods searchable at **https://genealogy.nationalarchives.ie**.

## Further census resources and population lists

Most of the Scottish censuses from 1841–1901 are available in transcript form on several platforms. The 1911 census, which was imaged digitally and not microfilmed, remains exclusively available through ScotlandsPeople (p.38).

Ancestry and FindmyPast provide access to transcripts for the records from 1841–1901. I find that the FindmyPast transcripts tend to be slightly more accurate, but conversely that FindmyPast's source citations are extremely poor when compared to Ancestry. It is also worth noting that the transcripts on both platforms are incomplete, with information not provided for questions such as the number of rooms with one or more windows, whether the person enumerated was blind, deaf or dumb, or whether he or she was able to speak the Gaelic language (from 1891). On Ancestry the marital status of a woman is also not noted if she is in a household without her husband, making it impossible to tell if she is a widow or not. On a more positive note, if you find a person in a particular census, the menu to the right of the screen provides options to search additional censuses for which the platform believes results may be for the same person.

A small number of records for Scotland from 1851 can be found on TheGenealogist, from a 2% extraction of the records previously carried out in 1979 (selected from every fiftieth enumeration book). Census transcripts from 1881 for inmates and staff of Scottish poorhouses can also be freely accessed at **www.workhouses.org.uk/Scotland/ UnionsScotland.shtml**.

FamilySearch provides very limited access to information for the Scottish censuses from 1841–1891. Unlike searches for the rest of Britain, Scottish results are provided only for a single individual, and not the full household, and with the minimum of information only: name, census year, sex, age, birthplace, registration district, county and estimated birth year. The source citations also erroneously note the records coming from TNA and not the NRS. FamilySearch's presentation of the 1881 Scottish census is actually much less complete than the organisation's transcribed results for the same records as freely presented on ScotlandsPeople.

Transcripts for many census records from the Borders from 1841–1861 are freely available at ScottishIndexes. Results presented will provide links to other censuses for which the company believes the same individual has been found, but also additional information, such as whether a person is deceased by the time of a subsequent census (where known). It is also possible to look at previous and next households, and for some returns there is also a handy link to a map on the NLS maps platform (p.63), identifying where the property is located. A list of areas covered is available at **www.scottishindexes.com/coveragecensus.aspx**.

FreeCEN (**www.freecen.org.uk**) is a free-to-access volunteer-run project painstakingly transcribing records from 1841 to 1891. While its English returns are more complete for the latter censuses, Scottish coverage tends to favour 1841 and 1851, and to an extent 1861. The transcripts are of a very high standard. The 'Database Coverage' option of the home page menu details what has been transcribed.

The 1939 National Identity Register returns for Scotland, compiled on 29 September 1939 for the purposes of registration, exist in a computerised form but are not searchable online. The NRS offers an ordering service for extracts, with details available at **www.nrscotland.gov.uk/research/ guides/national-register**. If your Scottish ancestor or relative was south of the border at the start of the war, the English and Welsh register has been digitised, and can be accessed on Ancestry, FindmyPast and MyHeritage (see p.24), although information for anyone still alive will be redacted for privacy reasons.

There are several additional Scottish census-based resources that may be of interest. A Vision of Britain Through Time hosts census reports at **www.visionofbritain.org.uk/census** for 1801–1971, including population tables and statistics on subjects such as occupations, as does Histpop at **www.histpop.org** from 1851–1911. The latter also provides a unique snapshot illustrating just how widespread religious adherence had become in Scotland by the middle of the century, via the returns of the Religious Worship Census of 1851, taken alongside the main decennial census on 30–31 March. The Scottish returns were not as comprehensive as those in England, and most of the original schedules have not survived, but the report (accessible at **https://bit.ly/1851ReligiousScotland**) breaks down the number of congregations by denomination, providing a fascinating breakdown of each denomination across the country. Examples of known surviving returns from Morayshire can be read on my blog at **https://bit.ly/1851ScotsReligiousCensus**. For an interesting insight into the numbers of Scottish Gaelic speakers recorded in 1891, the first year to ask the question, visit **www.linguae-celticae.org/GLP_ English.htm**.

Census returns from 1801–1831 did not record the names of individuals in each household, but lists were nevertheless compiled from which the returned statistical information could be drawn. While very few of these lists are online, the NRS does provide a guide on what has survived at **www.nrscotland.gov.uk/research/guides/census-records/pre-1841-census-records**, which includes a page from the 1811 census for Dallas in Stirlingshire. An excellent online resource for the 1821 census from South Ronaldsay and Burray, within the Orkney Islands, is available at **www.southronaldsay.net/1821/**.

In 1755, the Reverend Alexander Webster carried out a national census of some 900 parishes. A published version of this exercise, which does not provide names but statistical information only, is available online at **www.nrscotland.gov.uk/files//research/census-records/websters-census-of-1755-scottish-population-statistics.pdf**.

An 'Inventory of Published pre-1841 Population Listings' can be consulted at the SAFHS website (p.14) for information about earlier census resources and substitutes, and a 'Scottish Censuses, Population Listings & Communion Rolls (mainly pre-1841)' list, as compiled by genealogist Kirsty Wilkinson, is also accessible at **https://bit.ly/listspre1841**.

In 1834 the Church of Scotland passed the Veto Act to try to stop the influence of landowners in the selection of parish ministers (p.78), a right granted to them in 1712 through the Patronage Act. On the back of this Act each parish compiled annual lists of heads of households in order to determine an electorate from the congregation to exercise the 'veto' against any such appointments, if it chose to do so. The Old Scottish website has made lists available for the first year in which such lists were gathered, 1834, and presented them in its 'Rolls of Male Heads of Families' collections for each parish (where such records have survived and/or been indexed).

Valuation rolls (p.40) from 1855–1940 can act as an effective census substitute between the decennial censuses and post-1911: the ward maps for the Glasgow rolls in 1913-14 are available at **www.theglasgowstory.com/ward-maps/**.

Very few Scottish electoral registers or voter lists are online, but Ancestry has records for Perth and Kinross, Fife, Aberdeen and Aberdeen City (p.106), while FindmyPast has offerings from West Lothian (p.150). To trace people in more recent times, visit **www.192.com** and **www.theukelectoralroll.co.uk**, where information can be sourced from contemporary electoral registers and directories.

## Directories

Post Office directories and other street and trade directories are a further effective resource to help plot the location of a family on a yearly basis, but they can also provide a great deal of information on the contemporary make up of an area, recording businesses and organisations, and in some cases even providing maps. Edinburgh's first directory was published in 1773, with Glasgow's first edition appearing a decade later in 1783.

The contents of such directories evolved over time. Early editions listed those in the gentlemanly and professional classes: merchants, landowners, ministers of the church and local council members, as well as members of the judiciary. If your ancestor was not from the wealthiest landowning or merchant classes, and was perhaps instead an agricultural labourer or a miner, the chance of him being recorded in these early volumes is virtually nil, although you may still find useful information, such as the names of local farms or mines which may have perhaps employed him. As a volume designed specifically for communication, you may even find detailed gazetteer accounts of many of the towns or villages being served, with descriptions of local industries, electoral ward descriptions, detailed fold-out maps, tide, ferry and tram times, and more.

The listings information in directories is presented in various ways, such as being arranged in alphabetical order, by profession, and by trades and occupations. People noted may be found under one or all listings, and so all should be consulted, not least because one listing may carry more details than another. In later volumes, the address section may also record the electoral wards which individual streets belonged to, making them a useful companion source for electoral register research. The names of streets with which they intersected might also be listed, which can be useful if trying to locate a street which was subsequently renamed or demolished.

The NLS, working in partnership with the Internet Archive, has digitised some 1,042 Post Office Directories (aka 'PODs') and presented them online on two separate platforms. The NLS has its own dedicated website available at **https://digital.nls.uk/directories/**, which hosts some 700 directories from 1773 up to 1911, the latter year having been chosen to respect an unofficial closure period mirroring that of the 1911 census. However, the Internet Archive has placed all of the volumes on its website in a special 'Scottish Directories' sub-collection within its NLS category, at **https://archive.org/details/scottishdirectories**. For some cities in Scotland you will find annual directories available up to the 1940s.

FindmyPast has its 'Scotland, Post Office Directories' collections, which contain a substantial number of volumes from across the country, with details of these listed at the bottom of the search page. The site's

*'Britain, Directories & Almanacs' database also hosts some additional volumes of interest, including the following:*

- Lanarkshire, Glasgow, Jones's Directory, 1787
- Scotland, Almanac Of Scotland, 1810
- Thom's Official Directory Of Great Britain & Ireland 1894
- Thom's Official Directory Of Great Britain & Ireland 1914
- Aberdeenshire, Aberdeen, Post Office Directory, 1936–1937
- Lanarkshire, Glasgow, Kelly's Directory, 1968
- Lanarkshire, Glasgow, Kelly's Directory, 1968
- Lanarkshire, Glasgow, Kelly's Directory, 1972
- Lanarkshire, Glasgow, Kelly's Directory, 1974

TheGenealogist carries only a small number of Scottish directories, located in its 'Trade, Residential & Telephone Records' collection, as follows:

- 1773–4 Edinburgh Directory
- 1783–4 Glasgow Directory
- 1787 Glasgow Directory
- 1849–1850 Glasgow Post Office Directory
- 1851–2 Glasgow Post Office Directory
- 1857–8 Edinburgh Leith Directory
- 1861–62 Glasgow Post Office Directory
- 1874–1875 Glasgow Post Office Directory
- 1877–1878 Edinburgh and Leith Post Office Directory
- 1882–3 Greenock Post Office Directory
- 1892–1893 Edinburgh & Leith Post Office Directory
- 1893–4 Perth & Perthshire Directory
- Post Office Glasgow Directory 1907–1908
- 1913–1914 Glasgow Post Office Directory
- 1914–1915 Glasgow Post Office Directory
- 1915 Orkney & Shetland Directory
- 1923–1924 Aberdeen Post Office Directory
- 1925–1926 Glasgow Post Office Directory
- 1930 (Circa) The Official Guide to Edinburgh
- 1930–31 Edinburgh & Leith Post Office Directory
- 1948–49 Aberdeen Post Office Directory

Ancestry has its 'UK, City and County Directories, 1766–1946' database, including directories from Aberdeenshire, Fife, Perth and Kinross, as well as its 'UK and US Directories, 1680–1830', which includes some early Scottish holdings for Edinburgh, Glasgow and Aberdeen. A standalone title on the site is 'Burntisland, Fife, Scotland, Directory and Yearbook, 1892'.

Ancestry also hosts the 'British Phone Books 1880–1984' collection, as sourced from the archives of British Telecom, containing some 1,780 telephone directories. This collection can be a little frustrating to search, and it may be easier to browse the relevant Scottish tomes by selecting the year range of interest, then the year and finally the volume of interest. The earliest edition with Scottish content appears to be for the year 1896.

## Land Registration

The registration of land transfers in Scotland post-1868 is today handled by Registers of Scotland (**www.ros.gov.uk**), with offices in Edinburgh and Glasgow. This Scottish Government agency offers a research service through its website, with digital copies of records from the Land Register and search sheets from the historic General Register of Sasines (listing historic transactions for a property) available for purchase. The Land Register has been in operation since 1981 and will effectively replace the General Register of Sasines by 2024.

Prior to 1868 the system of Scottish land registration relied on the recording of 'sasines' (pronounced 'sayzins'), a continuous system which started in 1617, although earlier registration records exist. There were three different types of sasine register: the Particular Register for

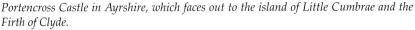

*Portencross Castle in Ayrshire, which faces out to the island of Little Cumbrae and the Firth of Clyde.*

each county, for registration of non-burgh-based lands in that county (abolished in 1868); the General Register, for the three Lothians and for lands to be registered in more than one county (reorganised as a national register from 1868); and the burgh registers, for registration within the royal burghs. A guide to these records can be found on the NRS website at **www.nrscotland.gov.uk/research/guides/sasines**.

The majority of historic sasines records pre-1869 are held at the NRS, accompanied by various printed abridgements from 1781, and historic 'minute books' for older records, summarising the transactions. While the records are digitised and accessible at the NRS, they have yet to be released by the archive online. Many records have been photographed by FamilySearch, however, and placed on its website, although the majority are locked for use by LDS members only, or for consultation at family history and affiliate centres. Those that can be consulted freely online will be identified within the relevant county sections in Chapter 5, and are summarised by ScottishIndexes at **www.scottishindexes.com/ learningsasines.aspx**, along with its own transcriptions coverage.

Another resource that can help is the Registers of Deeds from various courts in Scotland, although not a great deal is available online. A guide to the records at the NRS can be found at **www.nrscotland. gov.uk/research/guides/deeds**. Scottish Indexes is creating an index to the principal series, known as the 'Books of Council and Session', starting with records in 1769, and working back to 1661. Details on its project are available at **www.scottishindexes.com/learningdeeds.aspx**. FamilySearch hosts an 'Index to register of deeds, 1661–1696' at **www. familysearch.org/search/catalog/95952**, with several of the microfilms available digitally. Ancestry also has an index to the Register of Deeds from 1667 at **www.ancestry.co.uk/search/collections/indxrdeeds**.

The burgh register of deeds for Perth from 1566–1811 is digitised and available on Ancestry at **www.ancestry.co.uk/search/collections/ perthdeeds**, comprised of the 'Registers of Acts and Obligations from 1599–1805' (with gaps), and the 'Register of Deeds' from 1658–1666 and 1787–1811.

## Maps and Gazetteers

The NLS digital maps repository at **https://maps.nls.uk** offers over 200,000 high-resolution maps, covering not only Scotland, but also the rest of Britain, Ireland, Belgium, Jamaica, and the wider world. The site includes early maps dating back to the Scottish Reformation, Ordnance Survey maps, military maps, coastal maps, bathymetrical surveys, soil maps, estate maps, and much more. Its earliest map of Scotland is

'*Scotia, Regno di Scotia*', produced between 1558 and 1566, with the site also hosting important early collections such as Joan Blaue's *Atlas of Scotland* (1654) and William Roy's *Military Survey* (1747–55). In addition the platform holds Ordnance Survey maps at various levels from 1856–1961, and maps at county and town level dating back to the seventeenth century.

The NLS maps page permits the viewer to find and interact with the collections in a number of ways. Categories on the left of the page gather the collections into specific types and series, from Maps of Scotland to World Maps. Clicking on the individual menu items then provides information on the specific holdings within that category, with links. For example, clicking on 'Maps of Scotland' provides a list of records from 1560–1947, arranged by century in chronological order, which allows the user to dip in and out as required. This can be especially useful, in that when considered in chronological order, maps can reveal an incredible amount of detail about the contemporary and ever-changing landscapes within which our ancestors lived, as well as the changing historic boundaries of local authorities. The site also permits map searches through its 'Find by Place' category, and its 'Georeferenced Maps', which allow you to explore between various layers of maps and imagery that have been 'georeferenced', ensuring that each place of interest is pinned to the same spot between map overlays, therefore allowing users to mix between them for different views, including a satellite overview.

Maps can also be searched by a known mapmaker, and the 'OS Sheet Records Viewer' displays sheet information for five series of Ordnance Survey maps for the whole of Britain from 1841 to 1991. The 'Map Categories' section also offers a range of maps further categorised by type, such as a Land Utilisation Survey for Scotland from the 1930s, Soil Surveys of Scotland from the 1950s to 1980s, Scottish coastal charts from the 1580s to 1900s, military maps, trench maps, estate maps and bathymetrical surveys of inland freshwater lochs in Scotland, from 1897–1909. The final section on the page hosts information on 'Special Viewers and Projects', such as projects depicting where Scots-Italians lived and worked in Scotland from 1890–1940, and the GB1900 project, listing almost three million place names on the Ordnance Survey six-inch-to-the-mile maps of Britain (1888–1913), among other fascinating topics.

Other platforms to carry historic Ordnance Survey maps include Old Maps (**www.old-maps.co.uk**) and A Vision of Britain Through Time (p.65). The GENMAPS page at **http://freepages.genealogy.rootsweb. ancestry.com/~genmaps/index.html** has an extensive collection of old maps for Scotland at town and city level in its Scottish section. The

ScotlandsPeople 'Maps and Plans' section is also well worth exploring (p.43).

Modern maps online can be equally useful for research, with many places and streets named after historic settlements and farms no longer in existence. Google Maps (**www.google.co.uk/maps**) is by far the most useful, providing basic mapping, aerial photography and its 'StreetView' facility for viewing virtual environments at ground level. Other resources include Streetmap (**www.streetmap.co.uk**) and Bing's mapping facility (**www.bing.com/maps**).

To find out about the make-up of an area at any particular time, consult one of the many gazetteers freely available online. The NLS has a series of digitised nineteenth-century topographical and Ordnance Gazetteers available at **https://digital.nls.uk/gazetteers-of-scotland-1803-1901/archive/97491608** and on the Internet Archive at **https://archive.org/details/scottishgazetteers**. The A Vision of Britain Through Time site at **www.visionofbritain.org.uk** also hosts gazetteer and map resources for much of the country, including descriptions of places from John Bartholomew's *Gazetteer of the British Isles* (1887), among others. Samuel Lewis's two-volume *Topographical Dictionary of Scotland* is another excellent resource from 1846, hosted on the British History Online website at **www.british-history.ac.uk**, while an additional contemporary gazetteer is Undiscovered Scotland, available at **www.undiscoveredscotland.co.uk**.

Perhaps the most useful contemporary gazetteer-based accounts are the first two Statistical Accounts of Scotland, as recorded between 1791–1799 and 1834–1845. These accounts, based on a series of standardised questions, describe every parish in the country. They cover a vast range of subjects, including the names of principal landowners, the size and character of the population, the industries followed, the places and denominations of worship attended, the history of the parish, and even botanical information about native species. The best presentation online is from the University of Edinburgh's EDINA service at **https://stataccscot.edina.ac.uk/static/statacc/dist/home**, with both a free-to-access version and a subscription version available with enhanced search features. Additional free-to-access copies of the accounts can be found on Google Books and on Electric Scotland (p.70).

ScotlandsPlaces (p.14) also carries digitised copies of Ordnance Survey Name Books, noting the origins and spellings of many place names in the country. For a database of Scottish Gaelic place names see **www.ainmean-aite.org** (also accessible at **www.gaelicplacenames.org**), which includes recorded pronunciations in Gaelic of the places listed.

For the earliest history of Scotland's parishes, the Bannatyne Club published the two-volume *Origines Parochiales Scotiae: the Antiquities Ecclesiastical and Territorial of the Parishes of Scotland* in 1851. Both volumes can be consulted on the Internet Archive.

## Newspapers and Books

Newspapers are a fantastic resource for adding flesh to the bones of our ancestors' lives, with many indexes and digitised collections available online to assist. In addition to announcing various life events through their intimations sections, newspapers also carry stories concerning individuals of interest. The British Library receives a copy of every newspaper published in Scotland, as well as the rest of the UK, with an online guide to its holdings available at **www.bl.uk/collection-guides/ newspapers**.

In the 1980s, a cataloguing project of newspaper holdings across Britain and Ireland was commenced through a massive British Library-led initiative entitled NEWSPLAN, and its successor project NEWSPLAN 2000. Ten regions participated in the project, with the Scottish results hosted on the NLS website as the 'NEWSPLAN Scotland' project at **www. nls.uk/about-us/working-with-others/newsplan-scotland**. In addition to providing lists of titles microfilmed across the country through its 'NEWSPLAN 2000 Project' page, the site also provides a useful 'Guide to Scottish Newspaper Indexes', with a region-by-region breakdown of all known indexes for titles, either found online or at the National Library and local libraries, archives and other institutions.

The NLS also provides free access to Scottish residents to many digitised newspaper collections (p.11), as part of its licensed digital collections:

- Seventeenth and eighteenth-century Burney Collection Newspapers
- British Library Newspapers, Parts 1 & 2
- Access UK & Scotland Newspapers (local newspapers, mostly twenty-first century coverage)
- Infotrac Custom Newspapers (including thirty-three Scottish local titles)
- Scotsman Digital Archive, 1817–1950
- Times Digital Archive, 1785–2010

Many other libraries, including elsewhere in the UK, will also permit access to licensed digital collections. For those unable to subscribe, the

Scotsman Digital Archive is also available in a subscription-based format at **https://archive.scotsman.com**.

The Burney Collection and the British Library Newspapers are collections that source material from the British Library, with the latter including searchable versions of nineteenth-century editions of the *Glasgow Herald*, the *Chartist Circular*, the *Caledonian Mercury*, the *Dundee Courier*, and the *Aberdeen Journal*.

A considerably more impressive resource utilising material from the British Library is the British Newspaper Archive (**www. britishnewspaperarchive.co.uk**). This is a collaboration between the British Library and FindmyPast, and aims to host some forty million pages of content from across Britain and Ireland, with Scotland well represented. Access is via a subscription or by the purchase of credits. Note that it is possible to access the same records through a FindmyPast Pro subscription, however, if choosing to do so, be advised that the search interface on the British Newspaper Archive website is far superior to that on FindmyPast – so perhaps use this to carry out your free searches initially, and then access the images for the records found through your FindmyPast subscription.

Ancestry hosts some Scottish newspaper content, including a fairly substantial run of the *Dunfermline Journal* from 1851–1931, albeit with some gaps. Ancestry's other titles are mainly for Edinburgh, with fragmentary coverage:

- *The Edinburgh Chronicle* (1759–1760)
- *The Edinburgh Evening Courant* (1867–1869)
- *Edinburgh Advertiser* (1771–1829, with gaps, and 1909)
- *Edinburgh Weekly Journal* (1801–1808)
- *Edinburgh Courant* (Dec 1884)
- *Scotsman* (June 1945)

Ancestry also has two newspaper index databases for Perth and Fife:

*Perth, Scotland Newspaper Index Cards, 1809–1990* – a digitised version of the newspaper card index held at the A.K. Bell Library in Perth, Perthshire, referencing vital records intimations from *The Perthshire Advertiser, The Perthshire Courier, The Blairgowrie Advertiser* and the *Strathearn Herald*, with some additional references sourced from the *Kinross-shire Advertiser* and the *Perthshire Constitutional and Journal*. There is a gap in coverage between 1890 and 1920.

*Fife, Scotland, Cupar Library Newspaper Index Cards, 1833–1987* – a digitised version of a newspaper card index held at Cupar Library in Fife, referencing articles and intimations found in the *Coast Burgh* from Anstruther (8 Oct 1896–22 Dec 1898), the *Coast Burghs Observer* (1914 and 1917), the *Dundee Courier* (1926–1983), the *Fife Herald and Journal* (1890–1891), the *Fife Herald News* (1892–1893), the *Fife Herald* (1894–1986), the *Fife News* (1870–1909), the *Fife News and Coast Chronicle* (1910–1974), the *Fifeshire Journal* (1833–1893), the *East Fife Observer* (1917–1959), the *East of Fife Record* (1856 and 1858–1917), the *Pittenweem Register* (1850–1855, incomplete), the *Stratheden Advertiser* in Cupar (1853–1855, incomplete), the *St Andrews Citizen* (1977–1987), the *St Andrews Gazette*, Cupar edition (17 Jul 1869–24 Feb 1883), the *St Andrews Gazette*, Anstruther edition (29 Jul 1914–19 Feb 1915), the *St Andrews Times* (1937–38 and 1939–40), *The Fifeshire Express* in Cupar (4 Aug 1855–23 Jan 1856), and *The News* in Cupar (1858–1862).

The *Edinburgh Gazette* was first established in 1699, four years prior to the Union, and after an initially sporadic publication run for the next century it finally appeared regularly on a twice-weekly basis from 1793, continuing to the present day. As the official paper of record it notes various official announcements from government, but for the genealogist it is also useful for a variety of historic notices, including business announcements such as mergers, dissolutions and bankruptcies (cessio bonorum and sequestrations), military promotions, civic awards, name changes, estates claims and more. The title is free to view at **www. thegazette.co.uk** alongside editions for London and Belfast.

Google has its own free-to-access newspaper archive online at **https:// news.google.co.uk/newspapers**. Although overwhelmingly carrying content from the United States and Canada, several Scottish titles are also available. These are:

- *Glasgow Herald* (1806–1990)
- *Evening Times* (1953–1990, plus three earlier editions in 1914 and 1933)
- *Glasgow Advertiser* (1783–1801)
- *Bulletin and Scots Pictorial* (1951–1960)

The *Bulletin and Scots Pictorial* is listed simply on Google's list as *Bulletin*, but notes that coverage is apparently only available from 2 Jan 1957–28 Feb 1957. This is incorrect: a run of the paper is in fact online from 1951–1960. The easiest way to access the entire *Bulletin* collection is to simply click the following link: **https://bit.ly/BulletinScotsPictorial**.

When you click on the title of interest you will be taken to a new page where a series of thumbnail images for several editions are shown. These are initially arranged in columns by decade, but the frequency can be narrowed down to a day, week, month or year. You can also change the size of the thumbnails to small, medium or large. You can scroll along the page from left to right by clicking on it with your mouse and dragging it, or by clicking on the arrows at the top bar to the left and right.

If your ancestors lived in the Highlands, then Am Baile (**www.ambaile.org.uk**) has a superb, albeit incomplete, newspaper index on its site for the following titles:

*The Inverness Journal* (1807–1849)
*The Inverness Advertiser* (1849–1885)
*Scottish Highlander* (1885–1898)
*Inverness Courier* (1879, 1898–1901, 1920–1939)
*John O' Groat Journal* (1836–1887)
*Gairm* (1952–2002)

Janice Halcrow's impressive collection of Shetland newspaper transcriptions, including all BMD intimations from the *Shetland Times* from 1872–1990, is now hosted on FindmyPast in the following databases:

- Scotland, Shetland Newspaper Birth Index 1872–1990
- Scotland, Shetland Newspaper Marriage & Anniversary Notices 1872–2018
- Scotland, Newspaper Death Reports

Two newspaper collections of interest on TheGenealogist are *The Great War* (1914–1919) and *The War Illustrated* (1914–1919).

A great resource for the forerunners of newspapers, single-sheet broadsides posted in public places for the local community to read, is available from the NLS through a project entitled 'The Word on the Street', located at **https://digital.nls.uk/broadsides**. A collection of some 2,000 or so have been placed online under key headings, and are fully searchable. Through its 'Scottish History and People' page at **https://digital.nls.uk/gallery/category/scottish-history-and-people**, the NLS also offers the 'Broadsides from the Crawford Collection' for further broadsides from 1501–1897, and a collection of 'Chapbooks printed in Scotland' from the eighteenth and nineteenth century.

When it comes to books and journals online, the largest repositories of digitised content are Google Books (**https://books.google.co.uk**) and the

Internet Archive (**https://archive.org**). The content includes materials that are out of copyright, and cover just about every topic imaginable. Other digital libraries online include Scribd (**www.scribd.com**), the Hathi Trust (**www.hathitrust.org**), and Project Gutenberg (**www.gutenberg.org**).

The NLS also has a substantial number of digital books available, including its 'Scottish History Society' publications at **https://digital.nls.uk/scottish-history-society-publications**, with many other resources catalogued via its 'Scottish History in Print' collection at **https://digital.nls.uk/print**. The library also hosts a section of Antiquarian Books of Scotland at **https://digital.nls.uk/antiquarian-books-of-scotland/archive/120821910**, while its 'Publications by Scottish Clubs' resource at **https://digital.nls.uk/publications-by-scottish-clubs/archive/84240604** is also worth exploring.

Electric Scotland (**www.electricscotland.com**) is another online library of resources which describes itself as 'the largest and most comprehensive site on the history and culture of Scotland and the Scots at home and abroad'. The site carries thousands of books and other resources of interest, not just to the genealogist, but to anyone with a Scottish connection, including those with 'Scotch-Irish' (Ulster Scots) connections.

For academic publications, the JSTOR platform at **www.jstor.org** provides a substantial amount of free content, including historical journals such as *The Scottish Antiquary, or Northern Notes and Queries* from 1890–1903. Without a subscription only a small number of articles can be freely viewed, but free access is possible through the NLS licensed digital collections (p.11) and from other subscribing bodies.

Another useful resource for family history articles concerning Scotland in journals from the country and worldwide is the 'Periodical Source Index' (PERSI), as compiled quarterly by the Allen County Public Library in Fort Wayne, Indiana, USA, and presented on FindmyPast.

### Biographical Resources

There are several resources available online for those deemed to be historically 'of note' in their contribution to society.

One of the more fascinating collections is the NLS's 'Scottish History and People' section at **https://digital.nls.uk/gallery/category/scottish-history-and-people**. This includes many biographical collections, including the three-volume *Biographical Dictionary of Eminent Scotsmen*, and the *Histories of Scottish Families* collection. This latter collection hosts some 383 publications containing the family histories of many prominent families and clans from across Scotland, with a slightly expanded version also available on the Internet Archive's Scottish Family History section at **https://archive.org/details/scottishfamilyhistory**, with 430 volumes.

Matters regarding the laws and use of heraldry in Scotland are regulated by the Court of the Lord Lyon (**www.lyon-court.com**). Coats of arms have been digitised from the *Public Register of All Arms and Bearings* from 1672–1916 and made available at ScotlandsPeople (p.42). Many pre-1672 coats of arms, blazons and images can also be consulted at **www.heraldry-scotland.co.uk**. Various armorials can also be accessed freely within the above noted Internet Archive-based Scottish Family History section.

Several websites exist documenting the Scottish nobility, of both the 'old money' and 'new money' varieties. The subscription-based Burke's Peerage and Gentry (**www.burkespeerage.com**) contains *Burke's Landed Gentry Scotland* among its various offerings, as well as the various royal lineages of Britain. The 'Families Database' on Stirnet (**www.stirnet. com**) also provides pedigrees on many families from across Scotland and the British Isles, although after a brief preview appears your viewing will be interrupted to encourage you to subscribe to support the site. The free-to-access The Peerage site (**www.thepeerage.com**) has many distinguished pedigrees compiled by New Zealand-based Darrel Lundy: you can search for families by surname, or by place name under the Scotland header on the 'Master Place Index'.

The *Oxford Dictionary of National Biography* (**www.oxforddnb.com**) contains over 60,000 biographies on the great and the good, as do *Who's Who* and *Who Was Who* (**www.ukwhoswho.com**). Both are subscription-based sites, but free access is available through the NLS licensed digital collections, and other subscribing institutions.

The official website for the British Monarchy is **www.royal.gov.uk**, which includes details on how to access the Royal Archives – a version of the site in Gaelic is available at **www.royal.uk/gàidhlig**. Information on early Scottish monarchs is available at both **https://en.wikipedia.org/ wiki/List_of_Scottish_monarchs** and **www.royal.uk/early-scottish- monarchs**. If your ancestors worked for the royals, FindmyPast carries various collections covering the period from 1526–1924.

For memorials to women who have played a key part in Scottish history visit **https://womenofscotland.org.uk**. The site includes a memorials map, and an A–Z listing of those commemorated.

## DNA testing
An increasingly important development for family history research, which can establish connections even when the documentary evidence

fails, is the use of DNA testing. DNA carries important genetic instructions for our cells on how to grow and function. We inherit different types of DNA from our ancestors in different ways, but all can be tested and the results used to try to find connections with 'genetic cousins' who may carry the same DNA signatures as ourselves.

The following can be tested for family history purposes:

*Y-chromosome DNA (Y-DNA)*: this is passed from fathers to sons only, and should therefore follow the surname line, making it particularly useful for one-name studies. Once tested, the results are presented as a series of numbers, which relate to specific points or 'markers' on the DNA chain. Comparison of these marker values on a database will show how closely or distantly someone else may be related to you.

*Mitochondrial DNA (mtDNA)*: mitochondrial DNA can only be passed on by a mother to her children, making it useful for following a maternal line of ancestry. However, while mtDNA has its uses in the genealogical world (it helped to confirm the identity of the English king Richard III from his remains), its slow rate of mutation makes it the least useful test at present for family history research.

*Autosomal DNA*: the most recent development in the genealogy testing world is that for autosomal DNA, which is inherited as a mixture from both parents. This type of DNA is located within one of our chromosomes within the cell nucleus, though not the sex chromosomes (i.e. the X or Y chromosome). Autosomal DNA is most useful for testing for connections within the last four or five generations, with the shared amount of DNA with a genetic cousin measured in 'centimorgans'. You may share DNA with earlier generations than this, but the amounts will usually be so small that they will be incredibly difficult to find a match for. As such, it can useful to be able to test older members of your family, such as aunts, uncles and grandparents, to try to push the genetic record a generation or two further back.

In addition to being able to look for genetic cousins, DNA results can also be used to predict ethnicity. However, a serious word of warning here: the descriptions of ethnicity can be markedly different from one DNA tester compared to those given by another, as they are based on genetic markers available through results as gathered by those firms. For this reason, ethnicity results on an individual platform over time may also change, simply because the pool grows from which such descriptions are derived.

Several companies now sell DNA tests. FamilyTreeDNA (**www.familytreedna.com**) offers Y-DNA, mitochondrial and autosomal tests, as well as combination packages allowing you to test for more than one form of DNA at a time. Its website hosts various tools, such as a chromosome browser, where you can physically see exactly which parts of your DNA you have in common with your genetic cousins, as well as projects for trying to establish connections with other testers. If you have already carried out an autosomal test with 23andMe, AncestryDNA or MyHeritage (p.24), FamilyTreeDNA will allow you to upload the results to its site for free, but you need to pay US $19 to unlock several useful features to gain maximum use from them, such as its chromosome browser. Although a powerful player, FamilyTreeDNA's site can be a little overwhelming for beginners.

MyHeritage.com offers an incredibly versatile DNA platform for autosomal DNA testing. It has a host of tools including an ability to link to the family trees of users with whom you share parts of your DNA, and as with FamilyTreeDNA, a handy chromosome browser. MyHeritage freely permits you to upload raw DNA data results from tests already taken through Ancestry, FamilyTreeDNA, 23andMe and Living DNA.

Ancestry's offering, called AncestryDNA (**www.ancestry.co.uk/dna**), concentrates solely on autosomal tests. It allows you to host your results on your Ancestry account and to establish connections with other testers. Ancestry does not permit raw data from other testers to be imported, but does allow you to download its results for addition to other platforms. Unlike other companies, however, Ancestry does not permit you to view your results with the aid of a chromosome browser, citing privacy concerns. For complete beginners, Ancestry's site is very easy to get to grips with, and offers useful tools for genealogists such as its ThruLines feature, which can help you to identify possible ancestors as identified through the trees of others to whom you have a DNA link.

LivingDNA (**https://livingdna.com**) specialises in testing Y-DNA, mtDNA and autosomal DNA within Britain and Ireland, which gives it an edge in terms of explaining ethnicity results. At the time of writing it was preparing its Family Networks feature to allow users to reconstruct a family tree from their DNA, and has launched a partnership with FindmyPast. LivingDNA permits uploads of raw data from AncestryDNA, 23andMe, MyHeritage and FTDNA.

23andMe (**www.23andme.com/en-gb**) also offers DNA testing facilities for Y-DNA, mtDNA and autosomal testing, as well as a DNA database to help search for matches. Additional services, such as DNA testing for health risks, are also provided.

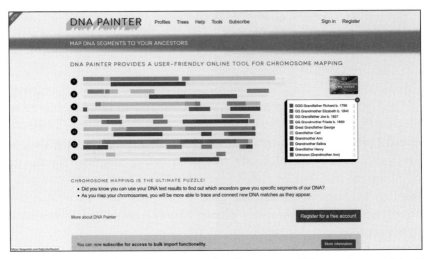

*The DNA Painter website allows you to visually portray which ancestors you inherit certain parts of your autosomal DNA from.*

Several other sites may be of use for DNA research. The International Society of Genetic Genealogy (**https://isogg.org**) has a useful 'ISOGG wiki' feature providing chapter and verse on all things technical with regards to DNA testing. DNA Painter at **https://dnapainter.com** is a fun tool which allows you to map out which parts of your genetic cousins' DNA match your own.

The University of Strathclyde runs short courses in genetic genealogy. Details can be found at **www.strath.ac.uk/studywithus/ centreforlifelonglearning/genealogy/geneticgenealogycourses research**. The university is also involved with the running of the Scottish DNA Project, as hosted on FamilyTreeDNA at **www.familytreedna.com/ groups/scottishdna/about/background**.

*Chapter 4*

# OCCUPATIONAL RECORDS

As well as creating a basic understanding of who our ancestors were and the locations in which they existed, it is also worthwhile pursuing the records of what they did for a living, to help us fully understand the daily struggles and achievements of their lives.

The most important starting point for occupational research will be the vital records of births, marriages and deaths, available on ScotlandsPeople (Chapter 2). Most early records will note the occupation of a child's father or an unmarried mother, while occupations for both parents will be listed in more recent twentieth and twenty-first-century records. Marriage records will usually note the occupations of both spouses, as well as their parents. Death records will state an occupation where there was one, with most records for widows also noting their deceased husbands' former occupations.

The decennial census from 1841–1911 is available on ScotlandsPeople, which will further record details of employment for all those working in a household every ten years. By researching your ancestors' vital events, as well as the records of their children and the censuses, you will be able to build up a work-life chronology for each individual, noting career progression or regression and their mobility in looking for work. Prior to civil registration, church records on the site are less reliable, but do on occasion provide occupational information.

The main genealogy vendor sites offer many collections on a variety of different occupations. Ancestry in particular has a dedicated platform at **www.ancestry.co.uk/cs/uk/occupations**.

Often a trade name may be presented in an old record that completely throws us, but handy tools for enlightenment include the ScotlandsPeople's list of occupations at **www.scotlandspeople.gov.uk/glossary** (select 'Occupations' under 'Term Type') and Hall Genealogy

Website's Old Occupation Names at **https://rmhh.co.uk/occup**. There are many possible trades within which your forebears may have worked, and it would be impossible to list them all.

The following sections detail some of the more common jobs and professions employing many across the nation.

### Farmers and Labourers

Most of us at some point will find agricultural labourers within our ancestry, with the country predominantly rural prior to the Industrial and Agricultural Revolutions. Many will have worked as farmers, ploughmen and farm servants (referred to in some parts as 'hinds'), dairy maids, and female servants. In addition to being recorded within the vital records and censuses, you might also find agricultural labourers mentioned within estate papers such as rental rolls, tacks (leases) and accounts. A guide to estate papers held at the NRS is available at **www.nrscotland.gov.uk/research/guides/estate-records**, although many other collections will also be found in local archives across the country, and at the NLS.

For a contemporary picture of where your ancestor might have worked in the 1790s and 1830s, consult the Statistical Accounts of Scotland (p.65), which will also help to identify the names of the relevant estate holders for whom they might have worked.

Several survey books were published in the late eighteenth century and early nineteenth century on a county-by-county basis for the Board of Agriculture entitled *General View of the Agriculture of the County of...* Each detailed the state of the agricultural industry in that area, including discussion on those working as labourers and farmers, the state of the land, and suggestions for improvements. Most are available to view on both Google Books and the Internet Archive; for example, *General View of the County of Inverness*, published in 1808, can be found at **https://bit.ly/GeneralViewAgricultureInverness**. A compilation of fourteen of the surveys from 1794, entitled *General View of the Agriculture of the Counties of Scotland, Issues 1–14* is available at **https://bit.ly/GeneralViewAgricultureScotland**, and covers Fife, Galloway, the Hebrides, Central Highlands, East Lothian, Midlothian, Southern Districts of the County of Perth, Renfrew, Roxburgh, Selkirk and Tweedale (Peebles), along with an account for the Isle of Man.

Another fascinating book concerning the rural workforce is *The Cottage, the Bothy and the Kitchen, an Inquiry into the Condition of Agricultural Labourers in Scotland*, by James Robb, editor of the *Scottish Farmer*, and published in 1861. Available at **https://bit.ly/AgriculturalLabourers1861**, it details the conditions of labourers based in East Lothian, Fife,

Forfarshire, Aberdeenshire and Rossshire, providing information on their earnings and general residential conditions.

If your ancestor was part of a Highland crofting community, he or she might have been interviewed as part of the Napier Commission, which investigated many complaints about rent increases, a lack of secure tenure and evictions. Its report was published in 1884, and is available online at **www.whc.uhi.ac.uk/research/napier-commission**.

Newspapers (p.66) also offer occasional glimpses into agricultural life, with local ploughing competitions, hiring fairs, and other rural activities within the agricultural calendar receiving regular coverage.

## Crafts, Trades and Merchants

Prior to the mid-nineteenth century, those working in trades or as merchants within Scotland's royal burghs had to serve time with masters as apprentices, before they could work independently as journeymen, and later progress to master craftsmen themselves. Records for apprentices include the tax payments made by masters upon the completion of their servants' indentures, available on Ancestry through its 'UK, Register of Duties Paid for Apprentices' Indentures, 1710–1811' collection. These can also be found via the 'Britain, Country Apprentices 1710–1808' collection on FindmyPast, and on TheGenealogist through its 'Apprenticeship Records' category (under 'Occupations'). Note that apprenticeships carried out within a family are omitted from these.

The records of the burghs and the trades incorporations, such as the weavers, dyers, butchers, wrights, hammermen etc, are usually held within local archives across Scotland, if they have survived: many can be located using the SCAN catalogue (p.8), or via online hosted catalogues for the relevant institutions in question. Some records are also held in Edinburgh at the NRS, which has a useful online guide at **www.nrscotland.gov.uk/research/guides/crafts-and-trades**.

For the right to work in a royal burgh, a craftsman or merchant needed a burgess ticket, or to become a 'freeman' of their relevant trade incorporation. This also allowed them the right to vote in burgh elections. FindmyPast's 'Scotland, Burgess & Guild Brethren Index' collection contains the names of some 64,000 inhabitants to hold such a ticket.

If your ancestor was based in Edinburgh, many apprentice and burgess records were previously made available online through the ScotsFind website, through downloadable PDF files. Although no longer active, a cached version of the site is available through the Internet Archive at **https://web.archive.org/web/20070127015608/http://scotsfind.org/**. FindmyPast hosts an alternative presentation of the records in its 'Scotland, Edinburgh Apprentices 1583–1700' database.

Additional burgh records for Dundee, Dumfries, Edinburgh and Glasgow are accessible via **www.scotsgenealogy.com/Links/Burgh Records.aspx**.

## Businesses

There are many records available in archives across the country concerning businesses established in Scotland, and their employees. The University of Glasgow's Scottish Business Archive is a useful first stop at **www.gla.ac.uk/services/archives/collections/business/**, with several collections concerning Scottish based firms from the eighteenth century to the present day. Of particular importance are records for shipbuilders on the Clyde, brewers and distillers, textiles firms and mining companies. The archive's website hosts many downloadable guides cataloguing holdings for each respective industry.

If your ancestor was in business, another major resource to check is the *Edinburgh Gazette*, which is freely available at **www.thegazette.co.uk**. Through this you will find details of business appointments, mergers, retirements and more. In particular, if your ancestor became bankrupt, through the Scots-based 'cessio bonorum' or 'sequestration' processes, you may find details of creditors' meetings. Sequestration records are held at the NRS: a guide to holdings is available at **www.nrscotland. gov.uk/research/research-guides/research-guides-a-z/court-of-session- records/sequestrations**. Once again, contemporary newspapers (p.66) will also carry details of business ventures.

Post Office Directories (p.60) are a useful resource for tracing a business, not just within listings but also in advertisements. In some cases these may include sketches of the wares manufactured, or images of factories or relevant premises.

## The Church

The most important biographical resource for Church of Scotland ministers is a series of volumes known as the *Fasti Ecclesiae Scoticanae*, initially published in 1866 and again in a revised format in the early twentieth century. The records are arranged by synods, and then by presbyteries, with a chronological list of appointments to each vacancy in the respective parishes going back to the Reformation of 1560. To identify which synod and presbytery a parish belongs to, consult the Statistical Account for the parish in question (p.65).

*The busy Parliament Square in Edinburgh is dominated by the High Kirk of St Giles Cathedral, where Protestant Reformer John Knox became minister in 1559.*

Each minister recorded is given a short biography accompanied by source details for the information provided. Ancestry hosts a database of the first edition at **www.ancestry.co.uk/search/collections/ scottishparishministers**; the records are fully searchable and are scanned in colour, with an additional browse option also available.

The Internet Archive hosts copies of the updated early twentieth-century editions, while the archive's Wayback Machine hosts a cached version of the Scottish Ministers Index at **https://bit.ly/ScottishMinistersIndex**, with updated editions of the first two volumes – these cover the synods of Lothian and Tweeddale (1914 edition) and the synods of Merse and Teviotdale, Dumfries and Galloway (third edition). On FindmyPast you will find the *Fasti* presented in a database entitled 'Church of Scotland Ministers 1560–1949', based on a later revised version of the work.

The 1904 publication *History of the Congregations of the United Presbyterian Church 1733–1900*, by the Reverend Robert Small, is available at **https:// bit.ly/UnitedPresbyterianChurchHistory**, while a limited preview of David M. Bertie's guide, *Scottish Episcopal Clergy 1689–2000*, is available on Google Books at **https://bit.ly/ScottishEpiscopalClergy1689-2000**.

If your minister served the Free Church of Scotland between 1843 and 1900, visit the excellent **https://ecclegen.com** platform for various research resources. A database of divinity students at Edinburgh's New College from 1843–1943 can be found on the University of Edinburgh's Historical Alumni site at **https://collections.ed.ac.uk/alumni/newcoll**.

The Surman Index Online at **https://surman.english.qmul.ac.uk/** lists Congregational Ministers predominantly for England and Wales, but records for Scotland are included also, with the names of many Presbyterians from the seventeenth and eighteenth century. For resources relating to the history of the Roman Catholic Church in Scotland, visit the Scottish Catholic Archives at **www.scottishcatholicarchives.org.uk**. The Salvation Army's International Heritage Centre in London has many historical resources at **www.salvationarmy.org.uk/international-heritage-centre** includes an online catalogue.

If your ancestor was a missionary, rather than a minister, consult the Mundus website at **www.mundus.ac.uk**, which lists over 400 separate collections of material relating to missionaries. The University of Southern California's Internet Mission Photography Archive at **http://digitallibrary.usc.edu/cdm/landingpage/collection/p15799coll123** is also well worth consulting, as is the catalogue of holdings for the School of Oriental and African Studies in London, available at **www.soas.ac.uk**.

## Teachers and Students

Prior to the nineteenth century most children were educated in parochial schools with school masters known as 'dominies' appointed and funded by the parish heritors and kirk sessions. A research guide from the NRS on its education record holdings is available at **www.nrscotland.gov.uk/research/guides/education-records**. Records for pupils are rare, but can be found in school logbooks in county archives if they have survived.

Ancestry hosts some school registers within the following collections:

• Perthshire, Scotland, School Registers of Admission and Withdrawals, 1869–1902
• Fife, Scotland, School Admissions and Discharges, 1867–1916
• Dunfermline, Fife, Scotland, Carnegie Music Institution Registers, 1910–1920

For university staff and student records you are advised to contact the respective institute's archive. The University of Edinburgh, for example, hosts its Historical Alumni Collection at **https://collections.ed.ac.uk/alumni**, with various lists available. FindmyPast has the following university databases:

- Scotland, University Of Aberdeen Alumni 1596–1900
- Scotland, University Of Edinburgh Graduations 1583–1858
- Scotland, University Of Glasgow Matriculations 1728–1858
- Scotland, University Of St Andrews Matriculations 1747–1897

The 'Aberdeen Roll of Graduates 1901–1925' and 'Glasgow University Matriculation Rolls 1728–1858' collections can be found online at The Genealogist (**www.thegenealogist.co.uk**), while an Aberdeen University Students Directory from 1933–34 is available on Family Relatives (**www.familyrelatives.com**). Ancestry also hosts a version of the 'Matriculation Roll of the University of St. Andrews 1747–1897' database, while the Scottish Genealogy Society hosts a page with links to various other resources at **www.scotsgenealogy.com/Links/Education.aspx**.

## Medical
For those who worked in the medical professions, Ancestry has a variety of searchable databases available with biographical content:

- UK, Dentist Registers, 1879–1942
- UK, Roll of the Indian Medical Service, 1615–1930
- UK, Physiotherapy and Masseuse Registers, 1895–1980
- UK, Medical and Dental Students Registers, 1882–1937
- UK & Ireland, Medical Directories, 1845–1942
- UK, Royal Navy Medical Journals, 1817–1857
- UK Surgeon Superintendents' Journals of Convict Ships, 1858–1867
- The Dunfermline Illustrated Almanac. Diary and Medical Guide 1868
- UK Medical Registers, 1859–1959

FindmyPast also hosts the 'Scotland, Glasgow Anderson's College Anatomy Students 1860–1874' collection, noting students who studied at Anderson College of Medicine, and a UK Medical Register from 1913. TheGenealogist further holds Medical Registers from 1861, 1873, 1875, 1888, 1891, and 1903, Medical Directories from 1848 and 1895, and a Dentists Register from 1937. In addition it hosts a '1727–1898 Roll of Army Medical Staff'.

The Royal College of Physicians in Edinburgh has Scotland's oldest medical library, with its Heritage platform at **www.rcpe.ac.uk/heritage** hosting a range of useful digitised resources, including a Medical Biographies section for some of the capital's more famous practitioners. The Index of Doctors in Scotland During the First World War is a separate platform from the college at **http://smsec.rcpe.ac.uk**, which provides a searchable database of physicians who registered with the Scottish Medical Service Emergency Committee as part of enrolment efforts during the conflict.

The Royal College of Surgeons of Edinburgh, established in 1505, has a Special Collections platform at **https://archiveandlibrary.rcsed.ac.uk/ special-collections** and a Surgeons database at **https://archiveandlibrary. rcsed.ac.uk/surgeons-database**. FindmyPast also hosts a separate 'Scotland, Fellows Of The Royal College of Surgeons of Edinburgh 1581– 1873' database. In the west, the Royal College of Physicians and Surgeons of Glasgow has a Heritage section at **https://heritage.rcpsg.ac.uk**, with an Archive catalogue at **https://archiveshub.jisc.ac.uk/rcpsg**.

ScotlandsPlaces carries Medical Officers of Health Reports for Scotland from 1891, with further reports freely available online from the Wellcome Library at **https://search.wellcomelibrary.org**. Search the term 'digmoh (scotland)'.

If your ancestor was a nurse, the 'Military Nurses 1856–1994' collection on FindmyPast includes records from various sources, including the Army Nursing Service, the Queen Alexandra's Imperial Military Nursing Service (QAIMNS), Royal Hospital Chelsea nurses, and the Scottish Women's Hospitals, founded in 1914 with funding from the National Union of Women's Suffrage Societies and the American Red Cross. The database also holds service information on nurses who served in the Second World War. Further information on those who worked in the Scottish Women's Hospitals and in other nursing roles can be found on the British Military Nursing site at **www.scarletfinders.co.uk**.

The St Andrew's Ambulance Association story is at **www.firstaid.org. uk/charity/about-us/history**, with the Women's Royal Voluntary Service (WRVS) history at **www.wrvs.org.uk/about-us/our-history**.

Find historic Scottish health records via the Hospital Records Database at **www.nationalarchives.gov.uk/hospitalrecords** or Discovery (p.9)

## Communications

The NRS hosts a substantial collection of records concerning Scotland's network of canals, although these do not list employees. A guide to the archive's holdings is available at **www.nrscotland.gov.uk/research/ guides/canal-records**.

The NRS also has a guide at **www.nrscotland.gov.uk/research/ guides/railway-records** detailing its substantial holdings from the major railway companies operating in Scotland. The Pensions Archive Trust site at **www.pensionsarchive.org**, which hosts many historical resources concerning occupational pensions in the UK, also includes a useful listing of railway-based pensions resources for Scotland as held at the NRS. Located at **www.pensionsarchive.org.uk/96/**, it provides catalogue references for Welfare Societies, Savings Banks, Superannuation, and Sick and Provident Funds.

Ancestry hosts a database of 'UK Railway Employment Records 1833–1956', which includes records from the London, Midland and Scottish Railway Company, and various other English-based services within which Scots might have worked. FindmyPast's 'British Army, Railwaymen Died In The Great War' database includes servicemen who attested for service from the Caledonian Railway, Glasgow and South Western Railway, Great North of Scotland Railway, the Highland Railway, North British Railway and Port Patrick and Wigtownshire Joint Railway, as well as other railway companies from across Britain and Ireland. The English-based National Railway Museum at York also has an impressive Fallen Railway Workers database at **www.railwaymuseum. org.uk/research-and-archive/our-research# first-world-war.com**, listing almost 21,000 railway workers who died in the First World War, with many Scots included.

The Railways Archive (**www.railwaysarchive.co.uk**) is a free online archive charting the development of railways across Britain. Scotland is well catered for, with the site including accident reports and maps and other resources. The history section of the Network Rail website at **www. networkrail.co.uk** also includes a searchable virtual archive, covering topics on stations, people, companies, tunnels and bridges/viaducts, with Scotland again included.

For those involved in the postal industry, Ancestry has its 'British Postal Service Appointment Books 1737–1969' collection, while the British Postal Museum and Archive has a guide on how to research postal family history at **https://bit.ly/PostalServiceFamilyHistory**.

## Mining

The Scottish Mining Website at **www.scottishmining.co.uk** is a true gem if your ancestor was a miner. The platform's resources are drawn from old reports, gazetteers and newspaper articles, with information offered on a variety of topics, including life in mining towns and villages, working conditions, accidents and strikes, housing, health and leisure, war memorials, and considerably more. The site focusses on the coal, iron and shale mining industries in Scotland, and includes a superb mining accident section with annual listings of fatalities from 1852–1944, as well as pre-1852 lists and post-Second World War records.

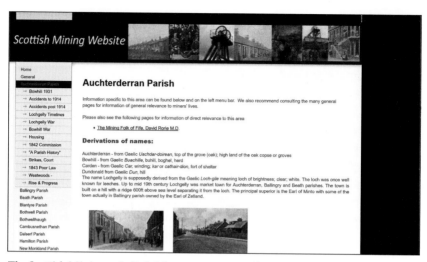

*The Scottish Mining website holds a treasure trove of useful resources.*

The Coalmining History Resource Centre (**www.cmhrc.co.uk**) includes the *Royal Commission of Inquiry into Children's Employment 1842*, a national database of mining deaths (including Scotland), with a handy page at **www.cmhrc.co.uk/site/maps/scotland/index.html** specifically hosting maps of Scottish mines.

The Hoods Family and Coalmining site offers resources for mining in Midlothian and East Lothian at **www.hoodfamily.info/coal/coalmining. html**, including details of historic Scottish and UK Acts of Parliament relevant to the industry, and resources for individual coal works from Duddingston to Sheriffhall.

The Women in the Pits platform at **https://freepages.rootsweb. com/~stenhouse/genealogy/coal/pbl/coalmain.htm** includes information from the Royal Commission Reports of 1842 into the coal mining industry, and a list of female deaths in Scottish mines from 1851–1914.

## Shipbuilding

If your ancestor worked in shipbuilding, it is worth bearing in mind that the workforce could be quite mobile, with workers as likely to migrate to Barrow or Belfast as they were to Glasgow. The UK and Irish censuses and vital records are therefore worth consulting if they seemingly disappear for short periods.

In terms of employment, the Scottish Business Archive (p.78) has useful guides, such as 'Ship building, ship repair and allied industries', 'Shipping companies' and 'Ships built on the River Clyde', detailing the records of many companies as held in their collections, predominantly for the twentieth century but with some nineteenth-century holdings.

The NRS also has a guide on its record holdings (within its Gifts and Deposit collections) at **www.nrsscotland.gov.uk/research/guides/shipbuilding-records**, as well as images at **www.nrsscotland.gov.uk/research/image-gallery/shipbuilding**. For records at Glasgow City Archives visit **www.glasgowlife.org.uk/libraries/city-archives/collections**, while additional localised holdings can be gleaned via the SCAN catalogue (p.8).

Information on over 35,000 Clyde-built ships can be found via the Caledonian Maritime Research Trust's Scottish Shipbuilding Database at **www.clydeships.co.uk**. The Aberdeen Built Ships Project at **www.aberdeenships.com** includes a database and history of some local shipbuilders.

## Theatrical

If your ancestor once trod the boards for a living then *The Stage* magazine from 1880–2007 should be a first port of call on the British Newspaper Archive (p.67).

The NLS's Scottish Theatre Programmes database at **www.nls.uk/collections/british/material-in-the-scottish-theatre-programmes-database** also contains information on over 13,000 programmes detailing performances, which can be searched by location and venue. The collection notably carries runs of programmes for the King's Theatre

*The NLS Scottish Theatre Programmes database allows you to search for materials which can be ordered up for viewing in Edinburgh.*

Edinburgh, from 1907, and the Royal Lyceum Theatre Edinburgh from 1883.

Bristol University's Theatre Collection has catalogues of holdings at **www.bristol.ac.uk/theatre-collection**, including many items for Scotland. The Theatre Database (**www.theatredatabase.com**) may be equally of use, charting performances and performers from ancient times to the twentieth century.

On the musical front, the Arts and Humanities Research Council has a database of musical concert programmes, including Scottish holdings, at **www.concertprogrammes.org.uk**.

## Photographers
For a database of photographers in Britain and Ireland from 1840–1940 visit the pay-per-view **www.cartedevisite.co.uk**.

The Scottish Highlander Photo Archive at **www.scottishhighlander photoarchive.co.uk** offers many images from portrait photographer Andrew Paterson (1877–1948) and his son Hector G.N. Paterson (1904–1988), both of whom were based in Inverness.

## Architects
If your ancestor was an architect, the Dictionary of Scottish Architects (**www.scottisharchitects.org.uk**) provides biographical information and job lists for all architects known to have worked in Scotland during the period from 1660–1980.

## Pensions
The Old Age Pensions Act of 1908 provided state pensions for the first time to those over seventy who earned less than £31 annually. With Scottish civil registration not commencing until 1855, the Scottish 1841 and 1851 censuses were moved to Edinburgh from London to assist applicants who required proof of age. Such records for Scots-born applicants have sadly not survived, but for those living in Scotland of Irish origin, applications requiring evidence from the Irish 1841 and 1851 censuses have survived, and are freely available online at the National Archive of Ireland's **www.genealogy.nationalarchives.ie**. The records can be searched by the applicant's name, the names of his or her parents, the census year searched, and by residency details.

Varying the search criteria for the 'Applicant's present address' yields many hundreds of Scottish-based applicants. For example, using the term 'Scotland' returns 387 applications, 'Glasgow' returns some 603 applications, 'Edinburgh' 626, 'Dundee' forty-seven, 'Ayr' four, and 'Aberdeen' just one. The term 'LGB Scotland' may be referred to in an applicant's Scottish address, short for 'Local Government Board Scotland'. Note that additional records held at PRONI can be searched on a separate site at **www.ireland-genealogy.com**.

For military pensions prior to 1914 and from the First World War, see p.91. At the time of writing, the Wellcome Trust is digitising Scottish First World War Pension Appeals Tribunal records, as previously catalogued under PT6 at the NRS – further information on these records is available at **http://britishgenes.blogspot.com/2018/01/scottish-ww1-pensions-appeal-records.html**.

## Military Service
Scotland has seen its fair share of wars across the centuries, both as an independent nation and as a constituent member of Great Britain and the United Kingdom.

### Pre-Union
One of the oldest documents detailing military obligations pertaining to Scots is the Senchus Fer n-Alban (History of the Men of Scotland), a tenth-century list derived from an earlier seventh-century record, detailing the genealogy of the Irish settlers of Dál Riata (Dalriada). This was the Gaelic kingdom which once straddled the Irish Sea from the east of Antrim in Ireland to Argyll in the west of Scotland, with the name 'Scotland' said to have been derived from the name of Irish migrants denoted as the 'Scoti' by the Romans. The document was drawn up to identify the strengths of the main branches of the settlers for military and taxation purposes. You can read more about it at **https://en.wikipedia.org/wiki/Senchus_fer_n-Alban** and see sample pages at **www.bbc.co.uk/scotland/history/first_census_scotland.shtml**. A summary of its contents is available at **www.duffus.com/Articles/senchus_fer_n_alban.htm**.

There are no surviving lists of soldiers who fought in Scotland's Wars of Independence, but The People of Medieval Scotland 1093–1371 website at **www.poms.ac.uk** is an impressive database of all known Scots from this period as identified in over 8,600 contemporary documents. A successor project, Community of the Realm in Scotland 1294–1424, at **https://cotr.ac.uk** is adding to this work. The databases cover the period of the emergence of Scotland as a nation, and in particular the Wars of Independence from 1296–1357, with many combatants and campaigns identified. A handy timeline from 1070–1331 at **www.poms.ac.uk/about/historical-introduction/** shows just how brutal much of the period was.

From 1603 to 1707, Scotland remained an independent country, but one which shared its monarchs with England and Wales, following the Union of the Crowns through James VI of Scotland (who became James I of Great Britain). It is within this period that the earliest surviving lists of Scottish soldiers are found, in a series of muster rolls dating from 1641 and the period of the Wars of the Three Kingdoms. The NRS has a helpful guide online identifying its military holdings for the period at **www.nrscotland.gov.uk/research/guides/military-records**.

During the seventeenth century there was immense persecution against those wishing to worship in the Presbyterian manner, leading in 1638 to the signing of the National Covenant, a protest document against Charles I's plans to introduce Anglican rites to Scotland. *The National Covenant: A List of Known Copies* is available at **https://archive. org/details/rschsv023p2stevenson**. This escalated into the struggle of the 'Covenanters' against the Crown, with a background to their story detailed at **https://bcw-project.org/church-and-state/sects-and-factions/ covenanters**. FindmyPast has a database entitled 'Scottish Covenanters 1679–1688'. The Records of the Parliaments of Scotland to 1707 (**www. rps.ac.uk**) may also assist.

### Fencibles, Militias and Volunteers

Following the Acts of Union in 1707, Scotland united with England and Wales, and from this point onwards the British army (p.90) became the main combined military force, with its records held today at TNA near London (p.8). Separate to this, however, there have also been several voluntary outfits such as Fencible, Volunteer and Yeomanry regiments.

The Fencibles were drawn up in the 1790s as a sort of home guard, designed to protect their immediate vicinities only, allowing the British army to go off to fight the Napoleonic French. For more on the Fencible Corps, read Ron McGuigan's excellent dissertation on the regiments, which includes a detailed list of units, at **www.napoleon-series.org/ military/organization/fencibles/c_fencibles.html**.

MyHeritage (p.24) hosts a database from a book entitled *Old Highland Fencible Corps: History of the Reay Fencible Highland Regiment of Foot, or Mackay's Highlanders, 1794-1802, With an Account of Its Services in Ireland During the Rebellion of 1798*.

Records of early Scottish militias can be found within sheriff and county court records, and so it is worth checking the holdings for the relevant counties through the NRS catalogue, although additional records are also held at TNA. In 1797 the Militia Act was passed, requiring a ballot of men aged between eighteen and thirty for compulsory service, with another Act in 1802 extending the age limit to forty-five. Again, many county archives have records of these ballots and of censuses carried out to ascertain who was eligible for service.

Ancestry hosts the 'Perthshire, Scotland, Militia Survey, 1802' collection at **www.ancestry.co.uk/search/collections/1642/**, which contains records for the burgh of Perth listing the names of males in every house aged between eighteen and forty-five. Additional Perth militia records are available at **www.culturepk.org.uk/archive-local-family-history/searchable-databases**. Forces War Records also hosts lists taken from the muster rolls of the Scottish (or North British) Militia at the start of 1800, and from the two Scottish battalions (5th and 14th) of the Army Reserve just prior to 1805 (see p.23).

Militia service attestation records for the period 1806–1915, catalogued at TNA in its WO 96 collection, are included within FindmyPast's 'British Army Service Records' collection and in Ancestry's 'Scotland, Ireland and Wales, Militia Attestation Papers, 1800–1915' database. They list new recruits' marital status, occupations, next of kin, prior service and medical examinations. FindmyPast also hosts a 'Scotland, Royal Volunteer Regiment Review 1860' database, noting those present at a review in Holyrood Park. The Volunteer Regiments were later integrated into the Territorial Army after 1907.

MyHeritage's 'British Militia Attestations Index, 1886–1910' and 'British Militia Attestations Index, Royal Garrison Artillery, 1872–1915' collections include the names of recruits from south and central Scotland, as well as many Scots who applied to serve with Irish based militias.

### Jacobites

The Union of 1707 was not popular in Scotland when passed, and resistance to it hardened through the Jacobite campaigns to restore the Stuart line, following the deposition of James VII (and II) in 1688 at the 'Glorious Revolution'. Several of the Jacobite campaigns are explored at **http://old.scotwars.com**. The culmination of the struggle was the 'Forty Five', the campaign from 1745–46 led by Charles Edward Stuart (Bonnie Prince Charlie), which ended so disastrously at Drumossie Muir at the Battle of Culloden.

Excellent online resources for the Forty Five include **www.jacobites. net**, which provides a good oversight and some biographical details of many of those who fought for Bonnie Prince Charlie. A ten-volume series of books entitled *The Lyon in Mourning*, a gathering of letters, journals and eyewitness accounts, was gathered in the immediate aftermath of the campaign by the Episcopalian minister Reverend Robert Forbes. These were later edited by Henry Paton in 1896 for the Scottish History Society, and republished in 1975 by the Scottish Academic Press. An online presentation of this is available via the NLS at **https://digital.nls.uk/print/transcriptions**, while a series of Jacobite prints and broadsides is available at **https://digital.nls.uk/jacobite-prints-and-broadsides/archive/74466725**.

*The Glenfinnan Monument at Loch Shiel, commemorating the landing of Prince Charles Edward Stuart on 19 August 1745, and the start of the Forty Five.*

FindmyPast hosts the 'Scotland, Jacobite Rebellions 1715 and 1745' database, with documents drawn from TNA in England, as well as a collection entitled 'Scotland, Jacobite Histories 1715–1745', with material drawn from twenty-three separate publications.

### The British Army

Many Scottish regiments have served with the British Army. The Internet Archive provides a useful regimental guide from 1901 at **www.archive.org/details/cu31924030726503**, entitled *The Regimental Records of the British Army: a Historical Resume Chronologically Arranged of Titles, Campaigns, Honours, Uniforms, Facings, Badges, Nicknames etc.*

Several regimental museums in Scotland commemorate the country's military heritage, each with their own web platforms offering a range of resources:

- The Royal Scots Regimental Museum **www.theroyalscots.co.uk**
- The Royal Scots Dragoon Guards Museum **www.scotsdgmuseum.com**
- The Museum of the Royal Regiment of Scotland **www.theroyalregimentofscotland.org/collection**
- The King's Own Scottish Borderers Regimental Museum **www.kosb.co.uk/museum**
- The Highlanders' Museum **www.thehighlandersmuseum.com**
- The Gordon Highlanders Museum **https://gordonhighlanders.com**
- The Black Watch Castle & Museum **www.theblackwatch.co.uk/castle-and-museum/the-black-watch-museum**

- Royal Highland Fusiliers Museum **www.rhf.org.uk**
- The Cameronians (Scottish Rifles) **www.cameronians.org/museum**
- Argyll and Sutherland Highlanders Museum **www.argylls.co.uk**

Some of these, such as the Gordon Highlanders Museum, offer a family history research service through their localised holdings. The Association of Scottish Military Museums is a body which represents several of these museums, and has a Facebook page at **www.facebook. com/AssociationScottishMilitaryMuseums**.

The Scottish Military Research Group is a charitable body which works on many commemoration and roll of honour projects for Scottish-based regiments, which are freely available at **www.scottishmilitaryresearch. co.uk**. The site also offers various research guides, including an excellent resource on how to identify Scottish military units from photographs, as well as a dedicated blog.

Historic service records of Scots serving within the British Army are held at TNA, ranging from attestation forms and muster rolls to records of payments and service. The archive has several useful guides to help you get underway with your research at **https://nationalarchives.gov. uk/help-with-your-research**. For soldiers serving prior to the First World War in 1914, the most useful records are those showing evidence of a soldier being discharged to pension or having served with a militia.

British soldiers could be discharged to pension through the royal hospitals at Chelsea, near London, or at Kilmainham, Dublin. A small number of soldiers were actually cared for at each institution, but in most cases soldiers would have been out-pensioners, receiving regular payments wherever they elected to settle after service. It did not matter which part of the British Isles your ancestor hailed from, the place of discharge was basically where you ended your service, with one of the hospitals then tasked with administering the relevant military pension: if you cannot find your ancestor in the records of one hospital, you should check the other. A pension was payable to soldiers who had served for more than twelve years in the army, and as such, the records will not contain information on those who left or died early in service, or who were killed in action.

If your ancestor was discharged at Chelsea, check the service and pension records which have been made available at FindmyPast as the 'British Army Service Records' collection. The records can provide brief service details, useful biographical details such as place of attestation and birth, physical descriptions and more. The records for soldiers discharged at Kilmainham are contained in a separate database on the site, 'British

Army Pensioners – Royal Hospital Kilmainham, Ireland, 1783–1822'. FindmyPast also offers a 'Scotland, Soldier Will and Testament Index 1602–1807' collection.

Ancestry equally hosts various British military records of use, including its 'UK, Royal Hospital, Chelsea: Regimental Registers of Pensioners, 1713–1882' collection, as well as medal rolls, army lists, and its 'UK, British Army Muster Books and Pay Lists, 1812–1817' collection. However, something to be aware of is that the Canadian branch of Ancestry has also digitised records from TNA, including regimental description books. These can be viewed on a British subscription and include:

- Canada, British Regimental Registers of Service, 1756–1900
- Canada, British Army and Canadian Militia Muster Rolls and Pay Lists, 1795–1850
- Canada, British Army Regimental Rolls of Non-commissioned Officers and Soldiers, 1806–1892

Despite the 'Canada' branding, these are most definitely British army records, and do not just include details for those who may have seen service in North America. For example, the Regimental Registers of Service 1756–1900 set lists an entry for William McEwan, brother to my four-times-great-grandmother Janet McEwan, noting that when he joined the 72nd Regiment of Foot he was 5ft 10¼in tall, aged 26 years and 3 months, had a fair complexion, long face, blue eyes and sandy hair, was born in 'Motherty' in Perthshire (in fact Madderty), and was a weaver by trade. He was enlisted in Perth on 1 March 1801 by an Ensign Wightman.

For officers in the British Army, the NLS hosts several monthly lists online at both **www.nls.uk/family-history/military-lists** and **https://archive.org/details/nlsarmylists**. Details of military promotions are accessible via the *Edinburgh Gazette* and *London Gazette* at **www.thegazette.co.uk**.

For the Napoleonic wars, the Peninsula Medal Roll is available at FindmyPast (1793–1814) and the Waterloo Medal Roll for 1815, while a roll call of mainly officers present at Waterloo is available at FamilyRelatives (some NCOs are also listed). Ancestry also hosts the 'UK, Waterloo Medal Roll, 1815' at **www.ancestry.co.uk/search/collections/1831**. If your ancestor served in the Boer War, visit **www.roll-of-honour.com/Boer** and **www.angloboerwar.com** for useful resources. Ancestry also hosts a 'UK, Casualties of the Boer War, 1899–1902' collection at **www.ancestry.co.uk/search/collections/1912**.

*First World War*

A useful overview of the First World War can be found via the Long, Long Trail at **www.longlongtrail.co.uk**. The site carries war diaries, dispatches, maps and more, and is accompanied by the Great War Forum at **www.greatwarforum.org**, with a range of topics under discussion from the conflict. If you are unsure which regiment or military service your ancestor might have served in, most birth and marriage records on ScotlandsPeople throughout the two world wars will note a person's usual occupation and in which capacity he or she may have been carrying out military service.

Just under forty per cent of British Army service records from the period have survived, the rest having been destroyed in a fire in Middlesex, England, in the Second World War, and have been catalogued by TNA under WO 363 and WO 364. Ancestry hosts these within two separate collections, 'British Army WWI Service Records, 1914–1920' and 'British Army WWI Pension Records, 1914–1920', while FindmyPast includes them within its 'British Army Service Records' collection. FamilySearch also holds the records under the title 'United Kingdom, World War I Service Records, 1914–1920', although the full records can only be accessed within an LDS family history centre.

FindmyPast further hosts the 'British Army Women's Army Auxiliary Corps 1917–1920' collection, various Royal Artillery records, and collections relating to those serving as nurses in the conflict. In addition are its 'Edinburgh Pals 1914–1918' and 'Glasgow Pals 1914–1918' sets, as well as its 'Scotland, Rolls of Honour 1914–1920'.

Further military records from the War Office, as held at TNA, have been digitised and made freely available through its Digital Microfilms facility at **www.nationalarchives.gov.uk/help-with-your-research/research-guides/free-online-records-digital-microfilm**.

The Lives of the First World War project was a crowdsourcing initiative from the Imperial War Museum and FindmyPast which ran from 12 May 2014 to 19 March 2019. Its aim was to encourage the public to collaborate and bring to life the stories of many of those who participated in the conflict, and to save these for posterity. The fruits of the project are now hosted by the IWM on a dedicated digital memorial platform at **https://livesofthefirstworldwar.iwm.org.uk**. The site allows you to search for information on individuals who participated through its 'People' filter, as well as providing the options to search for 'Stories' and 'Communities'. If I type in 'Glasgow', for example, and tick the 'Communities' filter box, I get the following results:

- Glasgow Necropolis
- Glasgow School of Arts
- The Hamiltons of Glasgow
- Anderson Brothers of Glasgow and Largo
- Alumni of the University of Glasgow
- Freemason of Glasgow
- Queens Own regiment of Glasgow Yeomanry
- Distant Relatives & Glasgow Academy Cadets 1902
- Glasgow Celtic Football Club in the First World War
- McCulloch Brothers
- Quintinshill Rail Disaster
- The Sellier Brothers from Trinidad, West Indies
- The Lodge of Glasgow St John 3bis
- Lodge St Vincent Sandyford No.553
- HMS *Perugia* (Q-1): 3 December 1916

Each of these is a community page with profiles of many who served in the war. Note that the Imperial War Museum's Collections and Research site at **www.iwm.org.uk/collections** also provides a great deal of information on how to research military ancestors from throughout the British Army's history, as well as several comprehensive online catalogues for its holdings.

Many additional wartime datasets are on the main vendor sites, and it is worth browsing through their respective catalogues and military sections to identify them. For example, FindmyPast, Ancestry and

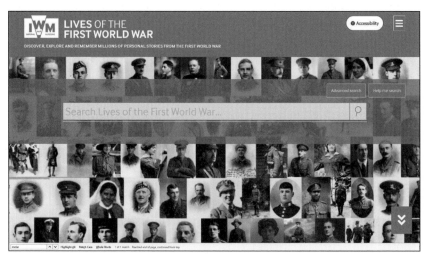

*The crowdsourced Lives of the First World War project is now hosted by the Imperial War Museum.*

MyHeritage have databases listing those injured who were entitled to the Silver War Badge from 1914–1920, while Ancestry, FindmyPast and TheGenealogist also host *De Ruvigny's Roll of Honour*, listing 26,000 officer deaths from all armed forces, and the *UK, Soldiers Died in the Great War, 1914–1919* collection, as produced by Her Majesty's Stationery Office (HMSO) in 1921. TheGenealogist offers the War Office's 'Weekly Casualty Lists', covering all ranks

Ancestry also hosts the 'British Army Medal Rolls Index Cards 1914–20' collection of almost five million records, listing soldiers and airmen who were entitled to receive a medal. The same cards are available via the TNA website, although only black and white copies of the fronts of the cards are supplied here, as opposed to Ancestry's colour scans of both sides (the backs of the cards sometimes reveal additional useful information). Forces War Records further offers a substantial amount of First World War material, as well as for other conflicts.

During the war the Princess Louise Scottish Hospital for Limbless Sailors and Soldiers was established in Renfrewshire in 1916, later to become known as the Erskine Hospital (and today simply as 'Erskine'). Thanks to a volunteer project with the Glasgow and West of Scotland Family History Society, and funding from the Wellcome Trust, its admission register from 1916–1936 has been digitised and indexed, and made freely available at **www.erskine.org.uk/patient-records-1916-1936**.

For those who died, ScotlandsPeople hosts its 'Soldiers and Airmen's Wills Collection', with additional wills for Scottish soldiers who served in Irish and other non-Scottish based British regiments available from **www.genealogy.nationalarchives.ie** and **https://probatesearch.service. gov.uk**. The Commonwealth War Graves Commission at **www.cwgc. org** lists the names of Scots men and women who gave their lives in the conflict and where they were buried or commemorated, including free to access documentation on the arrangements for their burials where available.

The Scottish National War Memorial, based in Edinburgh Castle, has a website at **www.snwm.org** which hosts an online Roll of Honour for Scots who served in both world wars, and subsequent conflicts. The University of Glasgow First World War Roll of Honour is available at **https://universitystory.gla.ac.uk/ww1-intro**.

The Western Front Association provides resources at **www. westernfrontassociation.com**, including a useful explanation about six million First World War pension record cards rescued by the organisation from destruction, which can be read at **www.westernfrontassociation. com/ancestry-pension-records**. Although searchable at Ancestry through its 'UK, WW1 Pension Ledgers and Index Cards, 1914–1923' collection, returning basic transcripts offered with some limited information, the actual images for the records can only be accessed on its sister site, Fold3 (**www.fold3.com**).

As part of its 'First World War 100' initiative, TNA's portal at **www. nationalarchives.gov.uk/first-world-war** has various record sets. Thousands of war diaries from France and Flanders (catalogued under WO 95) are included on its Operation War Diary platform (**www. operationwardiary.org**), as part of a mass crowdsourcing-based indexing and cataloguing campaign to capture names, places and events.

Many people became prisoners of war (POWs) during the conflict. The International Red Cross has digitised prisoner lists and has placed them online for free at **https://grandeguerre.icrc.org**. Volunteers who served with the British Red Cross can be searched for via **https://vad.redcross. org.uk**. Additional online resources for POWs are available at **https:// museumandarchives.redcross.org.uk/explore**. If your ancestor was a Scottish civilian POW interned in Germany (including many merchant seamen), visit The Ruhleben Story at **http://ruhleben.tripod.com** and Marcus Bateman's platform at **https://spw-surrey.com/mt9**. Others were confined at Kazerne Holzminden (**www.facesofholzminden.com**).

For the Second World War, TNA has very little army material available, its only significant holding being the Recommendations for Honours and Awards (1935–1990), which also contains details for RAF and Royal Navy personnel. Ancestry, however, has the 'UK Army Roll of Honour 1939–1945', compiled from various War Office sources between 1944 and 1949, and the 'UK British Army Prisoners of War 1939–1945' collection, with information on well over 100,000 POWs. Forces War Records has an excellent article detailing Second World War POW camps at **www.forces-war-records.co.uk/european-camps-british-commonwealth-prisoners-of-war-1939-45**.

*The Commando Memorial by Spean Bridge, commemorating those who served with the British Commandos in the Second World War.*

TheGenealogist hosts the 'Army Roll of Honour for World War Two', and has records from the Miscellaneous Foreign Returns, 1831–1964 (from TNA's RG 32 collection), which has notifications of deaths in Japanese and German POW camps, including names of those executed as prisoners. A detailed timeline of the war is available at **www.worldwar-2.net**, while **www.secondworldwar.co.uk** offers some background information on the key players and some general statistics.

### Domestic tragedies

One of the greatest domestic tragedies of the First World War was the Quintinshill Disaster of 22 May 1915, when a train carrying soldiers from the Royal Scots crashed near Gretna, with the loss of 230 people, including 210 servicemen, and the injury of a further 224 service personnel. As Scotland's worst-ever rail disaster, the incident is commemorated by the NRS at **www.nrscotland.gov.uk/research/learning/first-world-war/ quintinshill-disaster**, and by the Royal Scots at **www.theroyalscots. co.uk/quintinshill-train-crash**.

Equally tragic was the sinking of HMY *Iolaire* just after the war on 1 January 1919 as it approached Stornoway, Isle of Lewis, with the loss of 205 servicemen who were returning home. The incident is also covered by the NRS at **www.nrscotland.gov.uk/research/learning/first-world-war/the-iolaire-disaster-1919**, and elsewhere at **www.adb422006.com/ iolaire.html** and **www.virtualheb.co.uk/iolaire-disaster-western-isles**.

### Civilians at war

The Military Service Act of 1916 required all civilian men aged between 18 and 41 to register for possible compulsory military service, with this extended to the age of 51 by April 1918. Many sought exemption by appealing through the Military Tribunals system. While most records have not survived, those for the Lothians and Peebles were preserved as a representative sample, and are now digitised and available on ScotlandsPeople (p.42).

Also on the civilian front, the Devil's Porridge Museum site at **www. devilsporridge.org.uk** is worth a visit if your ancestors worked at the HM Factory Gretna munitions factory during the First World War.

In March 1941 Clydebank and Glasgow were blitzed by the Luftwaffe. The NRS holds many resources on the attack, which saw over 1,200 people killed, with a guide available at **www.nrscotland.gov.uk/research/ learning/features/the-clydebank-blitz-13-15-march-1941**. A list of casualties from Clydebank is available at **https://www.tommckendrick. com/code/casualties1.html**, while all who were killed in the attack are included in the Commonwealth War Graves Commission database, as part of the Civilian War Dead collection.

Forces War Records hosts a 'Home Guard Auxiliary Units Roll WWII' database, which includes nominal rolls from Scotland and Northumberland as recorded between September 1942 and October 1944 (sourced from WO 199/3388 at TNA). The site also hosts a 'Home Guard Officer Lists 1939–45' including those stationed in Scotland from 1940–1945 (as sourced from WO 409).

### The RAF

Taking to the air, the Royal Air Force started initially as the Royal Flying Corps, the history of which is outlined from 1914–18 at **www.airwar1. org.uk**.

Ancestry hosts the 'Great Britain, Royal Aero Club Aviators' Certificates 1910–1950' collection, which contains 28,000 index cards for pilots issued with licenses to fly. This offers the names and details of many who joined the RFC and the Royal Naval Air Service, as well as thirty-three out of thirty-four surviving photo albums containing images of airmen. The database includes 330 entries for pilots from Glasgow, 262 from Edinburgh, 78 from Dundee, 65 from Perth, 78 from Aberdeen, and 20 from Inverness-shire, with many other Scots recorded from other parts of the country.

FindmyPast offers the following RAF databases:

- British Royal Air Force, Airmen's Service Records 1912–1939
- British Royal Air Force, Officers' Service Records 1912–1920
- British Women's Royal Air Force Service Records 1918–1920
- Royal Air Force Lists 1919–1945
- Royal Air Force Muster Roll 1918

Ancestry also has the following:

- UK, Royal Air Force Airmen Records, 1918–1940
- UK, Royal Air Force Muster Roll, 1918
- Web: UK, Women's Royal Air Force Index, 1918–1920

Forces War Records (p.22) hosts a 'Royal Air Force Nominal Index of Airmen and Airwomen 1918 to 1975' which may help for post-1939 research.

A Roll of Honour for airmen who have died while serving with the Fleet Air Arm can be searched at **www.fleetairarm.com/fleet-air-arm-roll-of-honour.aspx**, mainly for the Second World War and onwards.

The RAF Museum (**www.rafmuseum.org.uk**) has many useful resources, including downloadable copies in PDF format of RAF Historical Society journals, details on the museum's resources, and online exhibitions such as Lest We Forget, which also includes a virtual Book of Remembrance. The site also has an interesting article on Proud Scots in the RAF at **www.rafmuseum.org.uk/blog/proud-scots-in-the-raf/**.

For a list of RAF squadron associations, and their contact details, visit **www.associations.rafinfo.org.uk/squadron.htm**, while a series of RAF lists from the 1920s can be consulted at FamilyRelatives, with information on all ranks from air marshal to pilot officer. RAF records can also be searched for on Forces War Records (p.22), while further Air Force lists for 1919, the late 1930s and most of the Second World War are available from the NLS via the Internet Archive (see p.11). For a useful list of RAF stations in Scotland, visit **https://en.wikipedia.org/wiki/Category:Royal_Air_Force_stations_in_Scotland**.

Many abbreviations found in RAF service records, and some RAF slang, can be decoded using **www.lancaster-archive.com/bc_abbreviations.htm**.

### The Royal Navy

Prior to the Union Scotland had its own naval force, the Royal Scots Navy, with a useful overview available at **https://en.wikipedia.org/wiki/Royal_Scots_Navy**.

Scotland also had an Admiralty Court from 1557–1830 with jurisdiction over maritime affairs on the high seas or in Scottish harbours, including criminal cases. The records can be searched via the NRS catalogue (under AC), while J.D. Ford's *A Guide to the Procedure of the Admiralty Court* can be read online at **www.scottishrecordsassociation.org/Scottish%20Archives%2018.web.9%20Ford.pdf**.

For the more recent Union period, the National Museum of the Royal Navy website (**www.nmrn.org.uk**) hosts useful material, while the Naval History site (**www.naval-history.net**) hosts an extensive collection including the history of ships and personnel, rolls of honour, and useful resources for the navy's story from the First World War to the Falklands.

TNA hosts many naval records collections on its site, with useful guides available via **www.nationalarchives.gov.uk/help-with-your-research/research-guides-keywords**. Many of the archive records are now digitised and available through Ancestry, with the site also offering third party indexes to collections hosted exclusively on the TNA site. These include:

- UK, Royal Navy Registers of Seamen's Services, 1848–1939
- UK, Naval Officer and Rating Service Records, 1802–1919
- UK, De Ruvigny's Roll of Honour, 1914–1919
- UK, Navy Lists, 1888–1970
- UK, Royal Navy Medical Journals, 1817–1857
- UK, Royal Navy and Royal Marine War Graves Roll, 1914–1919
- UK, Naval Medal and Award Rolls, 1793–1972
- Great Britain, Royal Naval Division Casualties of The Great War, 1914–1924
- UK, Commissioned Sea Officers of the Royal Navy, 1660–1815
- Canada, Registers of Prisoners of War, 1803–1815
- Web: UK, Royal Naval Seamen Index, 1853–1872
- Web: UK, Royal Naval Officers' Service Records Index, 1756–1931
- Web: UK, Women's Royal Naval Service Index, 1917–1919
- Web: UK, Royal Naval Volunteer Reserve Service Records Index, 1903–1922
- Web: UK, Royal Naval Reserve Service Records Index, 1860–1955
- Web: UK, Wills of Royal Naval Seamen Index, 1786–1882
- Web: UK, Royal Marines Registers of Service Index, 1842–1925

FindmyPast has the following:

- Britain, Royal Navy, Navy Lists 1827–1945
- British Royal Navy & Royal Marines Service and Pension Records, 1704–1919
- British Royal Navy & Royal Marines, Battle Of Jutland 1916 Servicemen
- British Royal Navy Allotment Declarations 1795–1852
- British Royal Navy Personnel 1831
- British Royal Navy Seamen 1899–1924
- British Royal Navy, Ships' Musters
- Royal Navy Officers 1899–1919

For earlier records, the Naval Biographical database (**www.navylist. org**) contains entries of many officers from 1660 to 1870, while a similar database of Commissioned Sea Officers from 1660–1815 is available at FamilyRelatives. Several Royal Naval lists can be viewed for free at the Internet Archive (**https://archive.org/details/nlsnavylists**), containing details on officers, while TheGenealogist also has some lists from 1822–1944 available.

TNA has a useful guide for researching ex-sailors who became Greenwich Pensioners at **www.nationalarchives.gov.uk/records/**

research-guides/royal-navy-rating-pension.htm. The archive also hosts a database listing everyone who served at Trafalgar at **www.nationalarchives.gov.uk/trafalgarancestors**, with service details and additional biographical notes where known, while The Age of Nelson website (**www.ageofnelson.org**) might also help.

If your connection is with the silent service, the Royal Naval Submarine Museum website (**www.submarine-museum.co.uk**) contains many photographic collections, an index of submarine losses, and a history of the service from its creation in 1901, as well as several online exhibitions.

A list of Scottish coastguards recorded in the censuses from 1841–1901 is included in the lists found at **www.genuki.org.uk/big/Coastguards**. TNA also freely offers additional Admiralty records on its Digital Microfilms facility (p.9), including 'Records of Service of the Coastguard 1816–1947'.

### Post-1945 Military Records

Following the war, many people ended up doing National Service, and serving in other conflicts. For comprehensive information on these campaigns, and additional resources such as regimental histories and rolls of honour, visit **http://britains-smallwars.com**.

If you wish to obtain copies of recent military service records still held by the Ministry of Defence, the UK Government's Veterans UK site at **www.gov.uk/government/organisations/veterans-uk** has all the relevant information, as well as a guide to claiming medals. For

*Post-First World War service records can be sourced via the British Government's Veterans UK platform.*

replacement medals, consult **www.awardmedals.com**. If your ancestor was the recipient of a Victoria Cross, consult Ancestry's 'UK, Victoria Cross Medals, 1857–2007' collection.

## Merchant Seamen

Shipping records for merchant seamen are held at archives across Scotland and the British Isles; Glasgow City Archives, for example, has a page on its holdings at **www.glasgowfamilyhistory.org.uk/Explore Records/Pages/Merchant-Seamen.aspx**. Additional records are held in many overseas countries such as Canada, which traded heavily with the UK.

The National Maritime Museum at Greenwich has useful guides on how to research maritime ancestors at **www.rmg.co.uk/national-maritime-museum**. TNA's Board of Trade records are available through the archive's online collection, with several guides and datasets accessible in the 'Military and maritime' category at **www.nationalarchives.gov. uk/help-with-your-research/**, including Merchant Seamen's Campaign Medal Records 1914–1918, and Merchant Shipping Movement Cards 1939–1945. A list of convoy movements in the Second World War can be explored at **www.convoyweb.org.uk**.

The Mariners site at **www.mariners-l.co.uk** has many guides on how to research merchant navy ancestors, fishermen, shipping companies and more. Lloyd's Captains' Registers, which give details on captains and mates serving on vessels whose details were transmitted to Lloyds, have been indexed by the Guildhall Library and made available at **www. history.ac.uk/gh/capintro.htm** for the period from 1851–1911. While many entries will need to be consulted at the library, some lists from 1800 are available at Google Books. Editions of *Lloyd's List* from 1801–84, and the *Shipping & Mercantile Gazette and Lloyd's List* from 1884–1914 can be searched on the British Newspaper Archive (p.67).

The Crew List Index Project is a major resource for research at **www.crewlist.org.uk**. Concentrating on the late nineteenth and early twentieth century, it holds various databases for those who served on board vessels, captained them or owned them.

FindmyPast hosts a 'Crew Lists 1861–1913' database, predominantly for crews registered in England and Wales, but with many Scots among them, as well as a 'Merchant Navy Seamen 1835–1941' collection. If your ancestor worked for the White Star Line, the vendor also offers White Star Line Officers' Books 1868–1934. Not to be outdone, Ancestry has equally impressive offerings in the form of its 'Glasgow Crew Lists 1863–1901', and the 'UK and Ireland, Masters and Mates Certificates, 1850–1927' database, detailing when certificates of competency were obtained.

Although predominantly a Northern Irish platform, Eddie's Extracts at **https://eddiesextracts.com/register/index.html** includes earlier Mercantile Navy Lists from 1845–50, noting the names of masters and mates who passed the relevant examinations. These are located under the Mariner Extracts menu tab on the home page, where you will also find entries from the Register of Deceased Seamen for the Shetland Islands from 1911–1925, and the Orkney Islands from 1911–1924.

The Maritime History Archive (**www.mun.ca/mha**) is focussed on Newfoundland, but has lots of British resources including a crew agreements database for 1863–1938 and an online catalogue. For maritime news from 1740–1837, including details of casualties and vessel movements, visit **www.cityoflondon.gov.uk/lloydslist**.

For resources concerning the Dundee-based whaling industry from 1756–1920 visit **www.fdca.org.uk/Whaling_Industry.html**. Accounts of the city's former seal and whaling industry are also available at **www.fdca.org.uk/Dundee_Seal_and_Whaling.html**.

Details about the Scottish Fisheries Museum library and archive can be found at **www.scotfishmuseum.org**, while the Scottish Maritime Museum offers information on its collections for research purposes at **www.scottishmaritimemuseum.org/research**.

## Law and Order

If your ancestor served as a policeman, the SCAN website has two useful guides at **www.scan.org.uk/knowledgebase/topics/policing_topic.htm** and **www.scan.org.uk/knowledgebase/topics/policerecords_topic.htm**, although few service record resources are available online.

Police Scotland has been a single unified force since 2013, but prior to this there existed many regional police forces across the country, which in turn evolved from earlier structures involving parish constables and policing arrangements within the burghs. The records for such agencies and forces will be held in local archives across the country, and should be searched for via SCAN, the NRS and local archive catalogues. One of the biggest surprises I ever made in my own research was to learn at Glasgow City Archives that my great-grandfather Robert Currie served with the City of Glasgow Police Force from October 1891 to September 1894. The reason for the surprise was that I was actually researching on behalf of a client for someone completely different and quite literally stumbled across his enlistment!

The Police Roll of Honour is at **www.policememorial.org.uk** and is searchable by surname, force and year. For the history of policing in Glasgow, visit the Glasgow Police Museum site at **www.policemuseum.org.uk**.

An overview of how to search for the records of the various Scottish courts, both civil and criminal, can be gained from various NRS guides at **www.nrscotland.gov.uk/research/research-guides/court-and-legal-records**.

There are many excellent legal dictionaries available online on Google Books and the Internet Archive, which can be of great assistance in understanding the crimes and offences prosecuted through Scots Law. These include:

- Barclay, Hugh (1855) *A Digest of the Law of Scotland, with Special Reference to the Offices and Duties of a Justice of the Peace (2nd edition).*
- Bell, William (1838) *A Dictionary and Digest of the Law of Scotland.*
- Blair, William (1834) *The Scottish Justices Manual; being an Alphabetical Compendium of the Powers and Duties of the Justices of the Peace within Scotland.*

Some select cases from the courts have also been published, with several volumes accessible online via Google Books and the Internet Archive.

Findmypast's 'Scotland, Court and Criminal Database' contains more than 130,000 records of Crown Office precognitions and High Court trial papers from 1801–1917, as well as records from the Fife Kalendar of Convicts, listing cases from 1708–1909. Ancestry also hosts a 'Fife, Scotland, Criminal Registers, 1910–1931' dataset.

Scottish Indexes has additional records of interest, including its 'Scotland's Criminal Database', with more than 150,000 High Court records, and its prison registers indexes, the coverage of which is outlined at **www.scottishindexes.com/learningprison.aspx**. The site also has a 'Scottish Paternity Index' recording paternity decrees from sheriff court records, while Old Scottish has a similar offering at **www.oldscottish.com/fathers-found.html**.

For additional details on prisoners in Scottish and other British prisons, consult **www.blacksheepancestors.com/uk**.

## The poor

Prior to 1845, the Kirk was responsible for making payments for poor relief to the destitute. Following the Poor Law Amendment (Scotland) Act the system changed, transferring responsibility for its administration to the state through a network of parochial boards, and from 1894, through parish councils. For those who were infirm, admission could be made to the poorhouse for 'indoor relief', but the majority of recipients received assessed payments instead through 'outdoor relief'. The system was eventually replaced upon the creation of the NHS in 1948.

For details of the poor law system in Scotland visit Peter Higginbotham's superb Workhouses site (**www.workhouses.org.uk**), where information on Scottish poorhouses can be sourced, including the location of relevant surviving records, along with transcripts of the 1881 census for each poorhouse. The NRS offers a further guide on poor law records at **www.nrscotland.gov.uk/research/guides/poor-relief-records**. An exceptionally useful guide to earlier holdings, created by Edinburgh-based genealogist Kirsty Wilkinson, is available as a downloadable PDF file at **https://bit.ly/PoorLawScotland**.

In many cases people were refused admission to the poorhouse if they did not have the right of settlement, gained by birth or by five years' residence within a parish. Many Irish and English applicants claiming relief or admission in Scotland were in fact put onto boats and sent back to Ireland or back over the border to England if no source for recompense could be identified: only a medical note could prevent a removal if such a decision was reached. The UK Parliamentary Papers website (p.11) contains detailed letters and annual reports from the second half of the nineteenth century with lengthy lists of people on a parish-by-parish basis who were so returned. If you cannot access the site, some rolls of people returned to Ireland from Scotland in 1867, 1869 and 1875–1878 are freely accessible at **www.raymondscountydownwebsite.com**. The records are particularly useful in that they detail to which parish in Ireland those being returned were sent, something that is not always the case in other Scottish records listing Irish folk, such as the census.

For an indication of the poverty affecting many areas of Scotland, consult the Medical Officer of Health Reports on ScotlandsPlaces, and through the Wellcome Library (p.82).

*Chapter 5*

# COUNTY BY COUNTY

Across Scotland there are many online projects created by local archives, libraries, museums and societies, which can readily help to embellish a family history. In addition there are many individual volunteer projects which can also assist with research into a range of issues, sometimes within quite niche areas, which can further shed light, and in some cases, even help to save a few pounds with free-to-access transcriptions.

In this chapter the aim is to provide an overview of localised resources for Scotland's historic counties, as well as her many islands, noting key archive and society offerings, genealogy vendor sites, local volunteer projects, interesting texts to be found on the Internet Archive and other library platforms, and additional niche resources specific to the area under discussion.

The aim is not to provide a complete overview – there are only so many pages in this book! – but to give a flavour of the enormous diversity of material available online for Scotland. In some cases I have also created links to useful resources that have long passed as active sites, but which have been resurrected using the Internet Archive's Wayback Machine (p.2).

To locate further holdings, use the gateway sites listed in Chapter 1, and keep an eye out on the genealogy news blogs for further releases.

## Aberdeenshire

The Aberdeen City and Aberdeenshire Archives site at **www.aberdeen city.gov.uk/services/libraries-and-archives/aberdeen-city-and-aberdeenshire-archives** carries a variety of free-to-access databases, such as a list of Loyal Macduff Volunteers from 1795, an Inverbervie Cess Book from 1757–1765, a Fraserburgh Police Court Book, Banff

Police Court Complaints, a List of Appeals before the Aberdeenshire Commission for Military Impressment 1757–58, Records of Certificates Granted for the Relief of the Wives and Families of Militia Men, and Militia Muster Rolls from 1803–4. The site also hosts research guides on burial records, church records, burgh records and education records, as well as an online catalogue.

The Aberdeen and North East Scotland Family History Society is one of the oldest in the country. Its website at **https://anesfhs.org.uk** hosts a 'Databank' with various free-to-access datasets, including Keithhall and Kinkell Register of Baptisms 1867–1928, St Nicholas Aberdeen Burials 1666–1793, an Aberdeen Stent Roll from 1669, St Nicholas Poorhouse Register 1779–1788 Index and Transcription, and St Nicholas Kirk Session Accounts 1602–1705. A monumental inscription index of 125,000 names from both published and unpublished sources (also covering Banffshire, Kincardineshire and Morayshire) is also available, while St Paul's Episcopal Baptisms 1720–1793 can be searched at **www.anesfhs. org.uk/databank/stpbapt/stpbapt.php**.

The Family History Society of Buchan's site (**www.buchanroots. co.uk**) has very limited resources online, but its site does list publications of interest for the area and includes a parish map for the Buchan area. An 1895 parish map for the whole of Aberdeenshire is also available at **https://bit.ly/Aberdeenshireparishes1895**, while Tim Lambert's history of the city is at **www.localhistories.org/aberdeen.html**.

The University of Aberdeen's Manuscript and Archive Collections catalogue can be searched at **www.abdn.ac.uk/special-collections/ manuscript-archive-71.php**. The site has many online data collections, including Rolls of Graduates from 1495–1970, a Roll of Honour for students, staff and alumni of the university who served in the two world wars, the MacBean Stuart and Jacobite Print Collection, the University of Aberdeen Oral History Archive, and Research Resources in Medical History. The Voices of Radicalism project is also offered here and at **www. abdn.ac.uk/radicalism**, documenting the fight for the vote throughout the nineteenth and early twentieth century. The university's Scottish Emigration Database at **www.abdn.ac.uk/emigration** lists some 21,000 passengers who sailed from Glasgow and Greenock, detailing voyages mainly between 1 January and 30 April 1923.

*The Armorial Ensigns of the Royal Burgh of Aberdeen*, written by John Cruickshank in 1888, is available on the Internet Archive at **https:// archive.org/details/armorialensignso00crui**. Electric Scotland hosts a transcript of Ebenezer Bain's 1887 book *A History of the Aberdeen Incorporated Trades* at **www.electricscotland.com/history/guilds**, while

ScotlandsPlaces hosts digitised copies of the first eight volumes of *Aberdeen burgh* registers (from the burgh of Old Aberdeen) which cover the period from 1398–1511.

The Aberdeen Built Ships Project at **www.aberdeenships.com** includes a database and history of local shipbuilders. Burial records for Aberdeen and much of the surrounding county are available on Deceased Online (p.23), while Ancestry hosts an 'Aberdeenshire, Scotland, Electoral Registers, 1832–1976' database.

Colin Milne's North East Scotland site has been saved by the Internet Archive and made available at **https://bit.ly/NEScotlandGenealogy**. The site includes militia records, newspaper extracts, graves photos, old school photos and more. The school headteacher's logbook for Pitsligo from 1874–1912 has been digitised by SCAN and made available at **www.scan.org.uk/researchrtools/schoollogbook.htm**, while a transcription of the school register from Daviot (1874–1923) is accessible at **https://bit.ly/DaviotSchoolRegister**. Resources for the history of families and communities in Glenbuchat can be found at **www.glenbuchatheritage.com**.

The village of Birse is featured at **https://bit.ly/BirseFolk** and includes censuses, strays, baptisms (1761–1779 and 1820–21) and marriages (1782–1799 and 1820–1826). A Register of Baptisms from 1763–1801 at Bairnie and Tillydesk can be examined on the Internet Archive at **https://archive.org/stream/scottishrecordso19scotuoft#page/n1/mode/2up**. Further parish records are available for Aberdeen, Chapel of Garioch, Cluny, Keig, Savoch and Strichen on FreeREG.

Although no longer being updated, resources for Kinnethmont, including censuses, old school photos and war memorial transcriptions, are available at **www.kinnethmont.co.uk**. Records for Upper and Lower Cabrach are available at **www.threestones.co.uk** and include war memorials, local songs, local books and more, while the Genealogy of the Cabrach site at **https://bit.ly/GenealogyCabrach** has records from various sources including censuses. Vital records for Strathdon are freely available at **https://sites.google.com/site/strathdonvitals**. The history of the Howe is at **www.mearns.org/history.htm**, with descriptions of several villages. For the village of Collieston visit **https://sites.scran.ac.uk/collieston/Home.html**.

The North East Folklore Archive, which focuses in particular on the farming and fishing communities of the region, is available at **www.nefa.net**. For the story of the North East's connections with the slave trade in the Caribbean, visit **www.abdn.ac.uk/slavery/index.htm**.

FamilySearch hosts the Secretary's Register of Sasines for Aberdeenshire from 1599–1609, and the Particular Register of Sasines from 1617–1629 and 1630–1660 at **www.familysearch.org/search/catalog/666861**.

## Angus

Previously known as Forfarshire until 1928, the history of Angus is dominated by the city of Dundee, which has its own dedicated archive. Its website at **www.dundeecity.gov.uk/archive** offers some documentary resources, including a List of Baillies, Provosts & Lord Provosts of the Burgh of Dundee from the year 1286–2017, and a detailed Subject Index of general holdings at the facility. In addition the site has several detailed research guides listing holdings for council records, official non-council records, church records and school records. The council also runs a historic images site entitled Photopolis (**www.leisureandculturedundee. com/photopolis**), which has some 5,000 old photographs of the city, with additional photographs of the city available via its dedicated Flickr platform at **www.flickr.com/photos/118069284@N05**.

Ably assisting the archivists are the Friends of Dundee City Archives, who have done some excellent work in transcribing many of the facility's holdings and placing them online at **www.fdca.org.uk**. Included are databases such as the 1801 census for Dundee, several burial collections including the Howff Cemetery, and additional resources such as the Lockit Book of Dundee, a nineteenth-century database of Dundee ships, poorhouse records for both the city and Liff and Benvie, Wesleyan

*The superb volunteer-based Friends of Dundee City Archives platform hosts many free-to-access records for the city.*

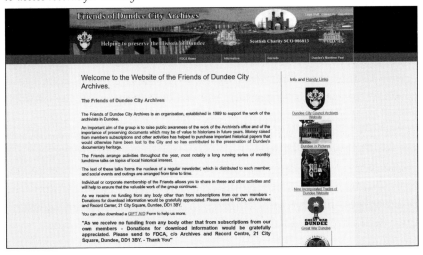

Chapel records, Cowgate school records (1899–1910), and much more. Maps of Dundee's cemeteries are available at **www.dundeecity.gov.uk/service-area/neighbourhood-services/environment/maps-of-the-citys-cemeteries**.

Information about Dundee City Library's Local History Centre can be found at **www.leisureandculturedundee.com/library/localhistory**, including information on its special collections, including its Tay Bridge Disaster holdings, the William McGonagall Collection, and the nineteenth-century Lamb Collection. Further information on the Lamb Collection is also available at **http://sites.scran.ac.uk/lamb**, with essays on subjects such as entertainment, cholera and crime and punishment, as derived from research into the collection compiled by Alexander Crawford Lamb (1843–97).

The Tay Valley Family History Society, also based in Dundee, has a catalogue of its holdings which can be downloaded from the 'Library' section of its platform at **www.tayvalleyfhs.org.uk**. The society also offers a dedicated discussion forum for members through its site, only entitled 'Tay Valley Bridges'. A separate group covering the Dundee area is the Abertay Historical Society, which freely offers several fascinating publications for download at **https://abertay.org.uk**, ranging from *Dundee and the American Civil War 1861–65* to *Martyrs in our Midst: Dundee, Perth and the Forcible Feeding of Suffragettes*.

Historic maps of Dundee, Forfarshire and the Firth of Tay are available at **https://bit.ly/Angusmaps**, while a maritime history of Tayside, including trade maps, essays on the flax industry, a mariners' database and more is available at **www.dmcsoft.com/tamh**. The Nine Incorporated Trades of Dundee site at **https://ninetradesofdundee. co.uk** contains transcriptions from thousands of historic documents concerning the burgh's various trade incorporations, as well as detailed information on the history of each respective trade.

For the story of Dundee in the First World War visit **www. greatwardundee.com/#fndtn-sixlives**, while the Dundee Women's Trail at **www.dundeewomenstrail.org.uk** celebrates some of the women whose lives have impacted on the city across time.

The Angus Archives site at **www.angusalive.scot/local-family-history** has very few resources online, but does provide details of its facility and an enquiry form for research requests. A superb blog on the local folklore of Angus is at **http://angusfolklore.blogspot.com**, while Unlock the Boxes at **https://bit.ly/UnlocktheBoxAngus** carries an interesting virtual exhibition on eighteenth-century life in Angus.

FreeREG includes some parish records for Arbroath, Barry, Dundee, Glamis, Kirriemuir, Monifieth and St Vigeans, while various burial registers sourced from Angus Council have been digitised by Deceased Online, with a page listing which areas have been included available at **https://bit.ly/DeceasedOnline-Angus**.

Resources for Monikie and surrounding areas are available at **www.monikie.org.uk/famhistory.htm**, including maps and hearth tax returns. Burials for Barry (1746–1800) are recorded at **https://bit.ly/BarryParishBurials**, while the Internet Archive has a reproduction of an 1895 book entitled *The Parish of Longforgan; a Sketch of its Church and People* available at **https://archive.org/details/parishoflongforg00philiala**.

For the University of Strathclyde's Declaration of Arbroath project, visit **www.strathgenealogy.org.uk/projects**.

## Argyll

Details for Argyll Archives, based in Lochgilphead, are available at **https://liveargyll.co.uk/facility/archives**, while the Local Studies page at **https://liveargyll.co.uk/local-studies** includes access to the Local Studies Catalogue. An earlier version of the council's Local Studies page is considerably more helpful at **https://bit.ly/ArgyllButeLocalStudies**, listing newspaper resources available at the council's various library branches across Argyll and Bute.

Highland Family History Society (**www.highlandfamilyhistorysociety.org**) covers Argyll, providing a publications list, and several indexes for

*Kinclochleven, North Argyll.*

burials, articles, the 1851 census, a Strays Index, and names featured in family trees held by the society. The Lochaber and North Argyll Family History Group (**www.spanglefish.com/lochaberfamilyhistorygroup**) further offers details of burial ground locations in Lochaber, as well as society newsletters.

The Friends of the Argyll Papers (Càirdean Phàipearan Earra-Ghàidheil) website at **www.friendsoftheargyllpapers.org.uk** offers a downloadable collection-level description of resources within one of the largest private archives in Scotland, that of the Campbell family of Inveraray Castle. The site also carries contact details for the archive, and information on how to join the Friends, while a separate Facebook page for the group is accessible at **www.facebook.com/friendsoftheargyllpapers**.

A transcription of a 1779 census of the Duke of Argyll's estates can be accessed at **http://web.ncf.ca/cv297/app1779.html**. If your ancestor was of the law-breaking kind, visit the Inveraray Jail site at **www.inverarayjail.co.uk** to look up the facility's prison records database.

Ralston Genealogy (**www.ralstongenealogy.com**) includes monumental inscriptions for some Kintyre-based cemeteries, as well as other local resources. For the Cowal peninsula, The Friends of Kilmodan and Colintraive site at **www.kilmodan-colintraive.org.uk** hosts gravestone inscriptions and histories for both churches. An abundance of records for Skipness parish, in the form of rent books, parish records, censuses, kirk session minutes, map and folklore, is available at **www.rootsweb.ancestry.com/~sctcskip**. For resources covering Knapdale, visit **www.knapdalepeople.com**.

A brief outline of the history of Appin is available at **www.appinhistoricalsociety.co.uk**. If you have connections to Barcaldine, Benderloch, North Connel or Bonawe, visit the Ardchattan Parish Archive at **http://ardchattan.wikidot.com/records** for various documentary resources, including censuses, valuation rolls and burial ground records. Some Ardchattan baptism records from 1820–54 are available on FreeREG, along with baptismal records for Kildalton and Oa (1725–1819) and Kilmeny (1820–54)

The history of Islay is outlined at **www.islayinfo.com**, including the tale of the clearances of the 1800s, while the Isle of Islay Gravestone Information Database has been preserved by the Internet Archive at **https://bit.ly/IslayGravestones**. A history for neighbouring Jura, along with genealogical research advice, is available at **https://isleofjura.scot**. Substantial resources for the Isle of Tiree are presented at **www.tireegenealogy.com**, while the island of Mull is also well served at **www.mullgenealogy.co.uk**, with a particularly useful burial ground map available at **www.mullgenealogy.co.uk/burialwb.html**. A further resource for Mull, Tiree and Coll is Mull Families at **www.mullfamilies. co.uk**. Parish records for Coll can be found at **www.collgenealogy.com/ OPR.html**, while assistance with Lismore research can be sought at **https://ardchattan.org.uk/argyllfamilies/lismore-family-history**.

The Isle of Gigha site at **www.gigha.org.uk** includes a history, an 1827 census, gravestone inscriptions, and history of the MacNeill family, while resources for Colonsay and Oronsay are at **https://colonsay.org. uk/history/colonsay-family-history**.

The Particular Registers of Sasines for Argyll from 1781–1895 can be accessed on FamilySearch at **www.familysearch.org/search/catalog/ 1047221**.

## Ayrshire

Ayrshire Archives is a joint service covering North, South and East Ayrshire local government authority areas. Its website at **www. ayrshirearchives.org.uk** hosts various catalogues, as well as a useful *Glossary of Burgh Records*, a list of available monumental inscription resources, and an excellent blog examining holdings from the collection.

North Ayrshire Council notes its available family history resources at The Townhouse in Irvine at **www.north-ayrshire.gov.uk/leisure-parks-and-events/culture-heritage/family-history.aspx**, and its local history materials at **www.north-ayrshire.gov.uk/leisure-parks-and-events/ culture-heritage/local-history.aspx**. This also includes access to the Ayrshire Working Lives database at **www.workinglives.org.uk**, with photographs of the county's industrial, commercial and agricultural heritage.

The Burns Monument Centre, which hosts East Ayrshire's archive resources, also conveniently hosts an on-site ScotlandsPeople service. Information on its available holdings is listed at **www.east-ayrshire. gov.uk/CouncilAndGovernment/BirthMarriageAndDeath/Scotlands-People/ScotlandsPeopleCentre.aspx**.

For a list of South Ayrshire genealogical resources at the Carnegie Library in Ayr visit **www.south-ayrshire.gov.uk/libraries/local-history. aspx**. This page also holds a free database entitled 'Births, Marriages and Deaths Archive Search from the Ayr Advertiser 1803–1835'. The South Ayrshire History blog from South Ayrshire Libraries is also worth perusing at **https://southayrshirehistory.wordpress.com**.

There are three family history societies in the county. The North Ayrshire FHS holds some microfilms and resources at Largs Library, with a list of materials detailed on its website at **http://northayrshirefhs.org.uk**.

The site for East Ayrshire FHS at **www.eastayrshirefhs.co.uk** has a discussion forum (members only) and parish list, while Troon@Ayrshire FHS's site at **www.troonayrshirefhs.org.uk** provides a cumulative index of memorial inscription transcriptions. The Alloway and South Ayrshire FHS sadly folded in 2015, but a handy parish map for the whole of Ayrshire, previously accessible on its website, has been preserved by the Internet Archive at **https://bit.ly/AyrshireParishes**.

Ayrshire Roots (two sites at **www.ayrshireroots.com** and **www.ayrshire-roots.co.uk**) is packed with resources including parish records, gazetteer descriptions and more. Ayrshire History (**www.ayrshirehistory.org.uk**) contains many fascinating articles on the county's history, while historic photos from the county are available at **https://homepages.rootsweb.ancestry.com/~ayrshire**. Historic maps for Ayrshire can be found at **https://bit.ly/AyrshireMaps**.

For North Ayrshire, the Three Towners site at **www.threetowners.com** has material for Ardossan, Saltcoats and Stevenston, including the 1819, 1822 and 1836 censuses, headstones information, newspaper intimations and poor relief database. The site also hosts various pages relating to the Ardeer Factory established by Nobel to produce dynamite. For historic photos and postcards of Largs, and descriptions of historic walks, visit **www.oldlargs.com**. A history of Skelmorlie and Wemyss Bay is available

*The Burns Mural at Ardeer Beach, Stevenston, commemorating Scotland's national bard, Robert Burns.*

at www.scribd.com/doc/1289541/Skelmorlie-Original-Walter-Smart-History-1968.

Some parish records from Beith, Dailly, Dunlop, Galston, Kirkoswald and Loudon are available on FreeREG, while a baptismal register for Stair (1862–1917) can be consulted at https://stairchurch.homestead.com, along with a headstone index. The parish church page for Ochiltree at https://ochiltreechurch.homestead.com includes a headstone index. The History section of the Maybole community website at www.maybole.org has the local 1841 and 1851 censuses and other resources. For the history of Barr, visit www.barrvillage.co.uk.

The Girvan and District Great War Forum is available on Facebook at www.facebook.com/Girvansfallen.

An Index to the Secretary's Register of Sasines for Ayr, from 1617–1660, is available at www.familysearch.org/search/catalog/610996.

## Banffshire

Many records from historic Banffshire are now looked after by Aberdeen City Council and Moray Council. The Banffshire Field Club website at https://banffshirefieldclub.org.uk provides a useful breakdown of where to find materials in each, as well as local libraries in Keith, Buckie and Macduff. The club's platform also provides a brief history of Banffshire, and of the club itself, which was established in 1880. For a further history of the county, visit www.electricscotland.com/history/moray/chapter15.htm.

The Aberdeen and North East Scotland Family History Society (p.107) covers Banffshire, while the Moray Burial Ground Research Group site at www.mbgrg.org includes details for some headstones found within cemeteries in the historic county. FreeREG includes some listings for the parishes of Aberlour, Alvah, Boyndie, Enzie, Fordyce, Forglen, Gamrie, Mortlach and Rothiemay.

FindmyPast hosts a database entitled 'Scotland, People of Banffshire & Moray 1150–1857'. The source for this is not listed, but it appears to be a searchable database based on publications by genealogist Bruce Bishop, including his extensive series of books, *Banffshire, the People and the Lands*. Further details on Bruce's books are available at www.scottishgenealogicalresearch.co.uk/publications.html.

The Keith and District Heritage Group website at http://kadhg.org.uk offers a history of the area and various resources, including an excellent monthly timeline of the area during the First World War.

An interesting paper on the use of aliases and patronymics in Upper Banffshire, by Stuart Mitchell, is available at https://bit.ly/

**UpperBanffshire**, which quotes many church records as part of its source material, naming many individuals.

An Index to the Secretary's and Particular Register of Sasines for Banff from 1600–1780 is available at **www.familysearch.org/search/catalog/666913**.

## Berwickshire

The Heritage Hub (**www.liveborders.org.uk/culture/archives/heritage-hub**) at Hawick, in historic Roxburghshire, hosts the archives for the four Scottish Borders counties, including Berwickshire. The centre also provides access to the ScotlandsPeople computer system. The service's catalogue, known as HUBCAT, is accessible at **www.calmview.eu/HUBCAT/CalmView**, but as this is not complete the archive advises that you should also consult SCAN (p.8) for further collection-level information on Scottish Borders based holdings. Information about libraries in Duns, Coldstream and Eyemouth can be found at **www.liveborders.org.uk/culture/libraries/our-libraries**, but note that the Local Studies Librarian for the Borders is based at Library headquarters in Selkirk.

Borders Family History Society has an interactive parish map at **www.bordersfhs.org.uk/b_shire.asp** with detailed guides to records held by both it and other repositories in Scotland. The society also has a research room in Galashiels.

Census records from 1841–1861 have been made freely available on ScottishIndexes (p.19), with many returns linked to maps at the NLS, as well as confirmed inter-census links to show family progressions across time.

FreeREG has listings for Abbey St Bathans and Foulden. An index to Berwickshire graveyard locations is online at **https://bit.ly/BerwickshireCemeteries**, while a one-place study for Whitsome at **https://bit.ly/Whitsome** has gravestone inscriptions, school records and the 1841 census for the parish. The kirk session book for Bunkle and Preston from 1665–1690 is available from the Internet Archive at **https://archive.org/details/sessionbookbunk00clubgoog**.

Monumental inscriptions from Eyemouth Cemetery and Eyemouth Old Kirk are indexed at **www.memento-mori.co.uk**, while the town's museum hosts a genealogy research service, affiliated to Borders FHS. Details are available at **http://eyemouthmuseum.co.uk**, in addition to several essays on local history subjects for the town.

A one-place study for the parish of Coldingham is available at **https://coldinghamoneplacestudy.org**, and includes various transcribed resources, such as lists of prisoners from 1842–1877, testificates from 1710–1744 (detailing the movement of people entering or leaving the parish), mortcloth records from 1694–1759, apprentice lists, taxation records, and other materials. An analysis of surnames in the parish is also presented, from the parish records.

A parish index for entries from the 1871 census for Berwickshire is available at **https://freepages.rootsweb.com/%7Econnochie/genealogy/census/bewcensus1871.html**.

The Berwickshire Lillies website at **www.berwickshire-lillies.co.uk** is a project celebrating the Lillie family of the Langton estate, where family members worked as blacksmiths. A list of strays from the Borders who settled in Victoria, Australia, from 1853–1895 is listed at **www.genuki. org.uk/big/sct/BorderStrays**, with many names from Berwickshire among them.

For an Index to the Particular Register of Sasines for the county from 1617–1780, visit **www.familysearch.org/search/catalog/414208**.

## Buteshire

The former county of Buteshire consisted of more than just the island of Bute, with part of the Scottish mainland to its north included as well as the two Cumbrae islands and Arran. *Topographical Dictionary of Scotland* descriptions from 1851 for areas within the former shire are available at **www.genuki.org.uk/big/sct/BUT**, with an additional gazetteer description from 1868 at **www.genuki.org.uk/big/sct/BUT/ Gaz1868.html**, and from 1896 at **www.genuki.org.uk/big/sct/BUT/ ButeshireGaz1896**.

The Local Studies catalogue for Argyll and Bute is accessible at **https:// liveargyll.co.uk/local-studies**, but many resources for the region remain held at a local level. FreeREG has listings for Bute, Cumbrae, Kilbride, Kilmory, Kingarth, North Bute and Rothesay.

The Internet Archive hosts a cached version of the former Bute Sons and Daughters Through the Centuries website at **https://bit.ly/ ButeSonsandDaughters**. This includes a surname index of those recorded in the 1841 census, a list of farms on the island, a history of Rothesay pier and more. A town plan for Rothesay from 1862–63 can be found at **https://sites.scran.ac.uk/townplans/rothesay.html**.

For the history of Mount Stuart House, and the Stuart family, visit **www.mountstuart.com**, with additional information about the property's world-renowned Bute Archive available at **www.butefamily. com/our-story/the-bute-collection**. Further general information on the heritage of the island can be found at **www.visitbute.com**. For a copy

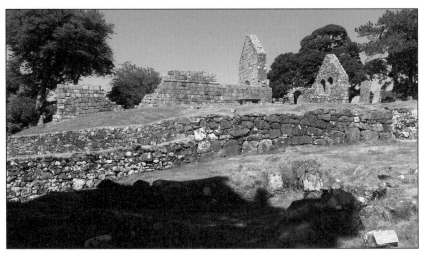

*St Blane's Church on the Isle of Bute, the origins of which trace back to the sixth century.*

of *The Isle of Bute in the Olden Time: With Illustrations, Maps, and Plans (1893–95)*, visit **https://archive.org/details/isleofbuteinolde01hewiuoft**.

The Isle of Arran Heritage Museum offers a genealogy service at **www. arranmuseum.co.uk/research/genealogy**. You can pay the museum's volunteers to carry out research on your behalf, or visit yourself, with access to the service included in your admission fee.

## Caithness

The Nuclear and Caithness Archives (**www.highlifehighland.com/ nucleus-nuclear-caithness-archives**) at Wick Airport host both the UK archive for the nuclear industry, as well as the historic county archives for Caithness, with records dating back to 1589. The website hosts an index to collections providing descriptions of holdings and relevant accession numbers, as well as a Caithness at War blog, with weekly posts detailing actions affecting the county during the Second World War.

A much older site at **www.caithnessarchives.org.uk** hosts additional resources, including a roll of honour for Caithness from the First World War. The Caithness War Memorials site at **www.caithness.org/atoz/ warmemorials/index.htm** also pays tribute to fallen sons from across the county.

Caithness Family History Society (**www.caithnessfhs.org.uk**) has limited offerings on its website, but it does provide a list of contents from past journals, a beginners' page and publications list, as well as details of a research service available for paid-up members. Highland Family History Society (p.111), also covers the county amongst its interests. For a parish map, visit **www.oddquine.co.uk/Genealogy/index.html**.

The history of various churches in the county is explored in detail at **https://churchhistorywick.weebly.com**, while graveyard records from Wick Cemetery, Berriedale Old, Berriedale Parish Church and Latheron can be sourced from Highland Memorial Inscriptions (**https://sites. google.com/site/highlandmemorialinscriptions/home**). The parish register of Canisbay from 1652–1666 can be consulted on the Internet Archive at **https://archive.org/details/parishregisterso67cani**.

FreeREG has listings for Bower, Canisbay, Dunnet, Halkirk, Latheron, Olrig, Reay, Thurso, Watten, and Wick.

For people with ancestry from the Theipland estates in Caithness, it is also worth consulting the Thiepland database hosted by Perth and Kinross Archives, which lists many tenants there (see p.141). If your ancestor was from John O' Groats, the *John O' Groat Journal* from 1836–1887 is indexed on Am Baile (p.69).

A list of ships in Caithness ports in the 1881 census is included at **www.angelfire.com/de/BobSanders/Scotland81-3.html**. The ships were berthed in Latheron, Thurso and Wick.

Various local history topics of interest can be read about at **www. caithness.org/history**, with the community platform also offering a discussion forum for the county at **https://forum.caithness.org**, which includes a substantial Genealogy section.

## Clackmannanshire

Clackmannanshire Archives is based at the Speirs Centre in Alloa, and is one of several heritage resources available at the family history centre there, which also offers access to the ScotlandsPeople service. A gateway platform at **www.clacks.gov.uk/culture/heritageservices** offers links to the archive service, the Clackspast Online Catalogue, the genealogy service and the Local History and Local Studies Service. The Local Studies page also provides details of several local groups, including Central Scotland Family History Society (p.148), Clackmannanshire Field Studies Society, Dollar Local History Group, Kincardine-on-Forth Local History Group, and Tullibody Local History Group.

Stobie's 1783 map of Clackmannanshire can be found at **http:// freepages.genealogy.rootsweb.ancestry.com/~russellsofwestfield**, along with maps of Westfield from 1845, 1848 and 1898, and census transcriptions for Westfield. Memento Mori (**www.memento-mori. co.uk**) hosts an index to monumental inscriptions for both Alva and Tillicoultry.

For a photograph of Clackmannanshire base church ministers circa 1890–1910, visit **www.genuki.org.uk/big/sct/CLK/Ministers/Ministers**.

*The Speirs Centre in Alloa offers access to the ScotlandsPeople platform, as well as Clackmannanshire Archives.*

Stobie's map of the county is also available through GENUKI at **www. genuki.org.uk/sites/default/files/media/images/big/sct/CLK/map.jpg**. A history of Menstrie Castle is available at **www.menstrie.org/hist_cas. html**, along with some photos.

The Internet Archive hosts an 1890 publication, *The Sheriffdom of Clackmannan; a sketch of its history with lists of its sheriffs and excerpts from the records of court, compiled from public documents and other authorities*, at **https:// archive.org/details/sheriffdomclack00wallgoog/page/n11**. The site also hosts forty-three separate twentieth-century Medical Officer of Health reports for the county, from 1896–1969.

### Dumfriesshire
Information about the Dumfries and Galloway Archives service, based at the Ewart Library in Dumfries, is available at **www.dumgal.gov. uk/article/15308/Local-archives**. The archive has a Council Archives Catalogue page at **http://archives.dumgal.gov.uk**, with several useful tools for ancestral research. In addition to the institution's dedicated catalogue, a series of Historical Indexes have been compiled by the Friends of the Archives of Dumfries and Galloway, covering the 1851 census, burgh records for Lockerbie, Moffat and Dumfries (including

jail books, bail bond registers, stent rolls and town council minutes), Customs and Excise records (shipping registers), and kirk session and presbytery minutes for churches in Dumfries, Mousewald and Troqueer.

The platform also offers an impressive newspaper catalogue, maintained by the Council's library service, which can be used to search through the *Annandale Herald, Annandale Observer, Dumfries and Galloway Standard, Dumfries Courier, Eskdale and Liddesdale Advertiser*, the *Galloway Gazette, Galloway News, Moffat News*, and *Stranraer and Wigtownshire Free Press*.

Dumfries and Galloway Family History Society hosts several resources on its platform at **https://dgfhs.org.uk**, including a newsletter index, pedigree charts, and certificate templates for transcribing birth, marriage and death records. The society has a research centre in Dumfries, and through a partnership with FindmyPast is now contributing records to the platform, including monumental inscriptions.

The Dumfriesshire and Galloway Natural History and Antiquarian Society site (**www.dgnhas.org.uk**) hosts an index to its *Transactions* periodical (1862–2009), and digital editions of the title, although many of these are large PDF files (up to 250MB), which would be unwise to download to a mobile device.

A list of Dumfriesshire parishes is available at **www.genuki.org.uk/ big/sct/DFS/parishes**. The Scottish Page at **https://homepages.rootsweb. com/~scottish** has links to many resources for the county as well as details of others with research interests there. FreeREG has records for Torthorwald, Tundergarth and Tynron.

For images of Dumfriesshire churches and graveyards visit **http:// homepages.rootsweb.com/~dfsgal**, while monumental inscriptions for many graveyards in the county can be found at **www.johnmacmillan.co.uk/ indx_cemetery.html**. Gravestone images from Canonbie are hosted at **www. flickr.com/photos/letsbikeit/sets/72157622608432658**, while memorials for Sanquhar Kirkyard can be consulted at **http://freepages.history.rootsweb. ancestry.com/~cdobie/sanquhar.htm**.

Scottish Indexes freely hosts valuation rolls for Annan, Applegarth, Caerlaverock, Canonbie, Closeburn, Cummertrees, Dalton and Dornock from 1896–97 on its Flickr page at **www.flickr.com/photos/ maxwellancestry/collections/72157649815538386**. The main Scottish Indexes site also provides free census records transcriptions for Dumfriesshire from 1841–1861.

A list of Provosts in Dumfries is available at **https://homepages. rootsweb.ancestry.com/~scottish/Provosts.html**. A history of the parish of Glencairn is at **https://archive.org/details/parishglencairn00montgoog**, and the history of the royal burgh of Annan at **www.annan.org.uk/ history/index.html.**

For irregular marriages carried out at Gretna, consult Ancestry's Gretna Green, Scotland, Marriage Registers, 1794–1895, at **www. ancestry.co.uk/search/collections/1636**, which contain about half of all known irregular marriages performed in the town during this period, as carried out by father and son team David and Simon Lang. Also for Gretna, the Devil's Porridge (**www.devilsporridge.co.uk**) deals with the history of munitions manufacturing at HM Factory Gretna in the twentieth century.

If your ancestors migrated overseas, a list of many born in the county who died in Canada is available at **https://homepages.rootsweb. ancestry.com/~scottish/D-GForeignBuried.html.**

For the Particular Register of Sasines for the Sheriffdom of Dumfries from 1672–1702, including the Stewartry of Annandale, visit **www.familysearch. org/ark:/61903/3:1:3Q9M-CS3Q-47MP-Y**. Subsequent registers for 1703–1732 and 1733–1780 are available at **www.familysearch.org/ark: /61903/3:1:3Q9M-CS3Q-43WX-T** and **www.familysearch.org/search/ catalog/611092**.

## Dunbartonshire

The historic county of Dunbartonshire is now administered by two authorities, West Dunbartonshire and East Dunbartonshire. The Glasgow and West of Scotland Family History Society covers the area (see p.131), while a list of the historic county's parishes can be viewed at **www.genuki.org.uk/big/sct/DNB.**

Information on the West Dunbartonshire Council Archives service is at **www.west-dunbarton.gov.uk/libraries/archives-family-history/ archives-collections**, with its holdings available for consultation at the Clydebank and Dumbarton Heritage Centres. The archive also offers a guide to Family History and Genealogy at **www.west-dunbarton.gov. uk/libraries/archives-family-history/family-history**. In addition, the site offers details of its oral history project on the region's industrial heritage, and a useful guide to place names in the area.

The East Dunbartonshire Archives Service covers the towns of Kirkintilloch, Lenzie, Bishopbriggs, Bearsden, Milngavie, Westerton, Lennoxtown, Milton of Campsie, Torrance, Baldernock and Twechar. Its page at **www.edlc.co.uk/heritage-arts/archives** offers some useful resources as downloadable PDF documents, including guides to graveyard records, house history, building plans, valuation rolls, tracing First World War ancestors, and a *Milngavie and Bearsden Herald WWI*

*Index* (in spreadsheet format). The council's local studies page at **www. edlc.co.uk/heritage-arts/local-history** is also worth exploring, as is its superb historic photo archive at **www.edlcimages.co.uk**.

The comprehensive Vale of Leven Story (**www.valeofleven.org.uk**) contains detailed histories of towns and villages in West Dunbartonshire, as well as a discussion board and essays on various aspects of local history.

For the town of Dumbarton, the More Than a Memory oral history project (**www.morethanamemory.org.uk**) has many recorded extracts in a dedicated multimedia section, as well as historic photos from the town – a highlight is cine film of the VE Day celebrations from 1945. A list of the civilian war dead from the Clydebank Blitz, during the Second World War, is available at **www.tommckendrick.com/code/casualties1. html**.

Memento Mori at **www.memento-mori.co.uk** has monumental inscriptions for Auld Isle (Kirkintilloch), Cadder, Campsie (cemetery and churchyard) and Kilsyth (cemetery and churchyard). Inscriptions for Rosneath, with a churchyard plan, can be viewed on the Internet Archive at **https://bit.ly/OldGraveyardRosneath**.

For the names of those on the war memorial at Bowling visit **www. happyhaggis.co.uk/dunbarton-bowlingWW1.htm**, and for Helensburgh visit **www.happyhaggis.co.uk/dunbarton-helensburghWW1.htm**.

A *Report on the Housing of Miners in Stirlingshire and Dumbartonshire* (1911) is at **https://archive.org/details/b21366329**.

## East Lothian

Until 1921, East Lothian was known as Haddingtonshire. For a list of parishes visit **www.genuki.org.uk/big/sct/ELN/ParishIndex**.

East Lothian enjoys the use of a combined Archaeology, Museum, Archive and Local History Services facility at the John Gray Centre in Haddington, with a combined online platform at **www.johngraycentre. org**. The site is a busy platform which can be a little difficult to navigate around, but the Archive Collections page at **www.johngraycentre.org/ collections/archive-collections-2/** hosts a link to various research guides, a Haddington criminal register, an index to the Haddingtonshire Militia and an index to the District Council Minutes. To search the General Registers of the poor for Dunbar, Innerwick, Oldhamstocks, Prestonkirk and Whitekirk, visit **www.johngraycentre.org/east-lothian-subjects/ society/poor-law-records**.

The Local History Centre Collections page at **www.johngraycentre. org/collections/local-history-centre** holds indexes for newspapers, including the *Haddingtonshire/East Lothian Courier, Musselburgh News, East Lothian News, Haddingtonshire Advertiser & East Lothian Journal, North Berwick Advertiser & East Lothian Visiter* (sic), *The Musselburgh Times & Scottish Central News, Allen's Original East Lothian, Berwickshire and Dalkeith Monthly Advertiser*, the *Musselburgh Monthly Reporter*, and the *East Lothian Oracle*. The East Lothian Council library catalogue is accessible at **https://capitadiscovery.co.uk/eastlothian**.

The Lothians Family History Society covers the area, and its website at **www.lothiansfamilyhistorysociety.co.uk** offers a list of parishes and a downloadable PDF-based Lothians Family History Society Library Catalogue detailing resources held at its research centre in Bonnyrigg. A Facebook page is also hosted at **www.facebook.com/people/Lothians-Fhs/100009903970976**.

A graveyard index and plan for St Mary's Church in Haddington is available at **https://bit.ly/StMarysHaddington**, while burial ground surveys for the parish of Traprain are at **www.ejclark.force9.co.uk**, with records for Prestonkirk, Stenton and Whittingehame. FreeREG has extensive coverage for the county, with records for Aberlady, Athelstaneford, Bolton, Dirleton, Dunbar, Garvald, Gladsmuir, Gullane, Haddington, Humbie, Innerwick, Morham, North Berwick, Oldhamstocks, Ormiston, Pencaitland, Prestonkirk, Prestonpans, Salton, Spott, Stenton, Thorntonloch, Tranent, Tynninghame, Whitekirk, Whittinghame and Yester.

The Dunbar Historical Society site at **www.dunbarhistoricalsociety. com** has a potted history and some media resources for the area, as well as an inventory of its collections. For a list of the Scottish officers captured at the Battle of Dunbar in 1650 visit **www.scan.org.uk/researchrtools/ military.htm**.

Information on friendly societies, incorporations, guilds and ancient orders in the county can be found at **https://bit.ly/FriendlySocieties**.

## Fife

The Fife Archives website at **www.onfife.com/libraries-archives/ archives** offers several useful resources for the family historian, including its fully searchable catalogue, and online guides to its electoral registers, police records and valuation rolls. The GENUKI Fife site provides a useful overview of the archive's holdings at **www.genuki.org.uk/big/ sct/FIF/libraries/Archives**. Additional pre-1891 materials concerning Culross and Tulliallan are also available at Perth and Kinross Archives (p.141), and for Arngask after 1891.

The University of St Andrew's Special Collections Department (**www. st-andrews.ac.uk/library/specialcollections**) has details on its various holdings, and links to pages such as the university's Photographic Collection, and its own dedicated archive catalogue.

Fife Family History Society (**https://fifefhs.org**) offers some free offerings on its site, under the Resources tab, such as a guide to the OPRs for Fife, and a guide to East Neuk tragedies, with additional offerings available to members only. Further records are accessible on older versions of the site, located via the Internet Archive. Tay Valley Family History Society (p.110) also takes in Fife. A parish map for the county can be found at **www.thefifepost.com/wp-content/uploads/2010/07/ Fife-Parish-Map-20151.jpg**.

There are several Fife specific databases available on Ancestry, including 'Fife, Scotland, Electoral Registers, 1914–1966', 'Fife, Scotland, Cupar Library Newspaper Index Cards, 1833–1987', 'Kirkcaldy, Fife, Scotland, Poor Law Records, 1888–1912', 'Fife, Scotland, Criminal Registers, 1910–1931', 'Kirkcaldy, Fife, Scotland, War Albums, 1899– 1916', 'Rosyth, Fife, Scotland, Dockyard Employee Books, 1892–1967', 'Burntisland, Fife, Scotland, Directory and Yearbook, 1892', and 'Dunfermline, Fife, Scotland, Carnegie Music Institution Registers, 1910– 1920'.

For biographical information on the great and the good, the Internet Archive hosts the *Biographical Dictionary of Eminent Men of Fife* (1866) at **https://archive.org/details/biographicaldic00conogoog** and *Lives of Eminent Men* (1846) at **https://archive.org/details/lives eminentmen00brucgoog**.

The published parish registers of Dunfermline from 1561–1700 can be consulted at **https://archive.org/details/scottishrecordso32scotuoft**. Directories, voters rolls, censuses, hearth tax records and more for Newport, Wormit, and Forgan are available at **www.twentytwoflassroad. co.uk**, while the Scoonie 1841 census is online at **https://bit.ly/ Scoonie1841**. FreeREG has records for Abdie, Cameron, Ceres, Cults, Dunbog, Dunfermline, Flisk, Kemback, Kennoway, Kettle, Kilmany, Kinghorn, Kinglassie, Leslie, Markinch, Moonzie, Scoonie, St Andrews and Wemyss.

A generic Fife site at **www.thefifepost.com** has many interesting sections on subjects such as the county's burghs, witches and trials, providing an interesting overview. Copies of the *Parochial Directory for the Counties of Fife and Kinross* from 1862 and 1866 are freely available on Google Books.

The history of the royal burgh of Burntisland is outlined at **www.burntisland.net** and includes the town's charter from 1541. A general history of Kincardine on Forth is recorded at **http://kincardinehistory.com**, with free resources in the form of the Tulliallan Kirkyard Records and Overton Cemetery Records.

The county's mining history is dealt with at **www.fifepits.co.uk**, which also includes the Kingdom of Fife Mining Industry Memorial Book database. For the history of the fishing industry, visit the website of the Anstruther based Scottish Fisheries Museum at **www.scotfishmuseum.org**.

## Inverness-shire

The Highland Archive Centre (Tasglann na Gàidhealtachd) in Inverness is home to the main archive repository for the Highlands, including Invernesshire, and has a dedicated platform at **www.highlifehighland.com/highland-archive-centre**, with information on the facilities available at the centre, as well as contact details. In lieu of a searchable catalogue, the archive offers *A Topical Index to Deposited Collections* at **www.highlifehighland.com/archives-service/deposited-collections/**, which usefully details a broad overview of catalogued holdings at series level.

*Am Baile (The Village) provides a major gateway to digitised resources concerning the Highlands.*

Information on the Family History Centre, which provides access to the ScotlandsPeople database, is further available at **www.highlifehighland. com/archives-service/archives/family-history-centre**.

By far the most comprehensive digital repository online for Inverness-shire is Am Baile (**www.ambaile.org.uk**), meaning 'The Village' in Gaelic, which covers much of the Highlands. The platform can be accessed in both English and Gaelic, and hosts various materials, both indexed and digitised, including newspaper indexes, maps, plans, photos, books and Gaelic resources, all for free.

Highland Family History Society covers the county, and its site at **www. highlandfamilyhistorysociety.org** includes an index for gravestones, a list of articles in the society's publications, members' interests, an 1851 census index and a further list of names found in compiled family trees submitted to the society. FindmyPast offers a collection entitled 'Scotland, Highland Free Church Birth & Baptism Index', based on transcripts recorded by Highland Family History Society, and which includes Invernessshire. The platform also offers a database entitled 'Scotland, Highland Poor Law 1845–1929', which includes records for Invernessshire, Moray, Ross and Cromarty, and Sutherland.

Highland Memorial Inscriptions (**https://sites.google.com/site/ highlandmemorialinscriptions/home**) has many cemeteries indexed, including that of Tomnahurich in Inverness, and a further forty-three cemeteries from across the county (the datasets may take a while to load). You can request full inscription details from the organiser, as well as images from the individual stones themselves.

The Old Home Town Image Archive (**www.theoldhometown.com**) includes historic images of Inverness, while the Scottish Highlander Photo Archive at **www.scottishhighlanderphotoarchive.co.uk** hosts thousands of historic black and white photos of individuals, the greatest proportion of whom came from Invernessshire.

A database of some pre-1850 Invernessshire vital records can be consulted at **http://freepages.genealogy.rootsweb.ancestry.com/~ked1/ Glen3.html**. FreeREG coverage is for Barvas, Cross Sub Barvas, Harris, Kilmonivaig, Laggan, Moy and Dalarossie, and St Kilda.

The Scottish Record Society's *Commissariot Record of Inverness : Register of Testaments, 1630–1800* dataset is located on Ancestry, but also for free on Electric Scotland at **www.electricscotland.com/history/records/ vol04.htm** and via the Internet Archive at **https://archive.org/details/ commissariotrec00grangoog/page/n7**.

The Moidart Local History Group (Comann Eachdraidh Mùideart) has various resources online for free at **www.moidart.org.uk/index.htm**, with a range of free resources grouped under themed headings such as Agriculture, Poverty in Moidart, Churches and Cemeteries, Gaelic, Courts and Police, and considerably more. Among these are offerings from the Glen Moidart papers (including estate rentals), and with some further holdings for members only, such as the 1841 census.

If your ancestor was from Urquhart, a database of Chelsea Pension records showing soldiers discharged from the British Army who gave the parish as their birthplace is at **http://freepages.genealogy.rootsweb. ancestry.com/~ked1/WO97.htm**.

The Invernessshire Emigrant Index (**http://freepages.genealogy. rootsweb.ancestry.com/~maddenps/INVEM1.htm**) lists many of those who sailed to New South Wales and Queensland. Databases of emigrants who sailed with the Highlands and Islands Emigration Society between 1852 and 1857 are also available through the Scottish Archive Network site at **www.scan.org.uk/researchrtools/emigration.htm** and on ScotlandsPeople.

For the stories of many forcibly evicted in the Highland Clearances, visit **www.theclearances.org**.

## Kincardineshire

The historic records for Kincardineshire (also known as 'the Mearns'), are today held by Aberdeen City and Aberdeenshire Archives (p.106), including records for the burghs of Banchory, Inverbervie, Laurencekirk

*Leanach Cottage, located on Culloden Battlefield near Inverness, was likely used as a field hospital during the battle in 1746.*

and Stonehaven. Kincardineshire is also covered by Aberdeen and North East Scotland Family History Society (p.107).

Images from many of Kincardineshire's churches and graveyards are available on Colin Milne's NE Scotland site, preserved on the Internet Archive at **https://bit.ly/NEScotlandGenealogy**. Additional images from churches across the county can be found on Lorraine Stewart's Kincardineshire Ancestors site at **www.kincardineshireancestors.co.uk/picture-gallery.html**.

The Portal to Portlethen site at **www.old-portlethen.co.uk** has many essays on the history of Portlethen, including subjects as diverse as privates and privateers, tee names (p.2), farming, and the church and clergy. For a history of Woodstone Fishing Station and St Cyrus visit **https://bit.ly/WoodstonStCyrus**.

FreeREG has some listings for Fordoun, while some census transcriptions from Garvock, Laurencekirk and Fordoun have been transcribed and made available at **https://freepages.rootsweb.com/~connochie/genealogy/kcd/1841kcdintro.html**.

*The History of Fettercairn* can be found on the Internet Archive at **https://archive.org/details/historyoffetterc00came**, while *A Concise Bibliography of the History, Topography, and Institutions of the Shires of Aberdeen, Banff, and Kincardine* is available at **https://archive.org/details/concisebibliogra00johnrich**.

For the Index to the Secretary's and Particular Registers of Sasines for the Sheriffdom of Kincardine 1600–1608, 1617–1657, visit **www.familysearch.org/ark:/61903/3:1:3Q9M-CS3Q-HSTV-V**.

## Kinross-shire
The historic county of Kinrossshire is today administered by Perth and Kinross Council. Perth and Kinross Archives' website at **www.culturepk.org.uk/archive-local-family-history/** has a catalogue and several online databases. Although focussed mainly towards the much larger county of Perthshire, the site does include an index called *Perthshire People & Kinross-shire Kin* at **www.pkc.gov.uk/article/3893/Perthshire-People-Kinross-shire-Kin**, which incorporates names from Kinross, and which can be accessed across a series of downloadable PDF documents arranged in alphabetical order.

*The Parishes of Perth & Kinross*, at **www.culturepk.org.uk/museums-galleries/collections/family-history-collections/the-parishes-of-perth-kinross/**, is another section of the council website which lists various holdings for the respective parishes at the Local and Family History

Department at the A.K. Bell Library in Perth. For a list of parishes in Kinrossshire, visit **www.genuki.org.uk/big/sct/KRS/parishes**.

Ancestry offers voters' rolls for the county as part of its 'Perth and Kinross, Scotland, Electoral Registers, 1832–1961' collection, while the 1841 census for the Kinrossshire parishes of Arngask, Cleish, Forgandenny, Fossoway and Tulliebole, and Portmoak, can be consulted at **https://bit.ly/Kinross1841**.

Kinross-based vehicle registrations, licenses and owners from 1904–1952 have been transcribed from records held at Dundee Council Archives and made available at **www.fdca.org.uk/Vehicle_Registrations.html**, which includes addresses for all those named.

For *The Place Names of Fife and Kinross*, visit **https://archive.org/details/placenamesoffife00lidd/page/n8**, while *A History of Fife and Kinross* is also available at **https://archive.org/details/ahistoryfifeand03mackgoog/page/n9**. The *Cambridge County Geography of Clackmannan and Kinross* is available at **https://archive.org/details/clackmannankinro01dayj/page/n8**.

The Internet Archive also offers several annual reports from the Fife and Kinross District Board of Lunacy from 1867–1873, providing statistical information on the running of Fife and Kinross District Lunatic Asylum.

Information about Kinross Museum can be found at **www.kinrossmuseum.co.uk**.

## Kirkcudbrightshire

Kirkcudbrightshire is today administered as part of Dumfries and Galloway, with the historic county's archives accessible through the region's archive in Dumfries (p.120). Dumfries and Galloway Family History Society also includes the historic county within its range of interests.

Additional local history and archive materials are held at the Stewartry Museum in Kirkcudbright, with further details at **www.dgculture.co.uk/venue/the-stewartry-museum-kirkcudbright/** and via its Facebook page at **www.facebook.com/The-Stewartry-Museum-468091149911060/**.

Two exceptionally useful sites for the Stewartry of Kirkcudbright are Stewartry Monumental Inscriptions at **www.kirkyards.co.uk**, with photographed and transcribed gravestone records for the parishes of Borgue, Buittle, Colvend, Parton, Rerrick, Tongland and Twynholm, and People and Places in Kirkcudbright at **www.kirkcudbright.co**, which includes searchable marriage and death notices from local newspapers among its offerings.

A modern map of Kirkcudbrightshire, along with some local family histories and researchers' interests is available at the Scottish Page at **https://homepages.rootsweb.com/~scottish/**, while free 1851 census transcriptions for part of the county are available at Scottish Indexes. A handful of cemetery records from twelve parishes within the county are also online at **www.johnmacmillan.co.uk/indx_cemetery.html**.

The Old Kirkcudbright site (**www.old-kirkcudbright.net**) contains a parish and burgh history, as well as valuation rolls, parish records such as OPR deaths from 1826–1853, stent rolls, census records for poorhouses in the county, and more. A history of Kirkcudbright parish church is also available at **www.kirkcudbrightparish.org.uk**, though the site hosts no records, although you will find some Kirkcudbright records of FreeREG. For the names of volunteers who joined the Urr Company Stewartry Kircudbright Volunteer Infantry on 16 July 1808, visit **https://donjaggi. net/galloway/urrvolunteers1808.html**.

A town history for Dalbeattie is available at **www.dalbeattie.com/ history**, which includes information on the granite quarries, port and industrial mills in the area.

The Internet Archive hosts *Kirkcudbrightshire and Wigtownshire* by William Learmonth (1920) at **https://archive.org/details/kirkcudbright shi00learuoft/page/n8**. Additional volumes on the platform with content for Kirkcudbrightshire include *History of the Lands and Their Owners in Galloway* (1906), the two-volume *The History of Galloway* (1841), and various editions of *The Transactions of the Journal of Proceedings of the Dumfriessshire and Galloway Natural History and Antiquarian Society*. Various editions of the *Annual Report of the Health and Sanitary Administration of the Stewartry* from 1923–1958 are also available.

For the Particular Register of Sasines for the Stewartry of Kirkcudbright from 1733–1780, visit **www.familysearch.org/search/catalog/611092**.

## Lanarkshire

The historic county of Lanarkshire is dominated by the city of Glasgow, but administratively is today divided between Glasgow, North Lanarkshire and South Lanarkshire councils. A parish list for the county is available at the Glasgow and West of Scotland Family History Society site at **www.gwsfhs.org.uk**, along with the society's library catalogue. The Lanarkshire Family History Society site at **www.lanarkshirefhs.org. uk** also offers an online discussion forum open to the public.

In Glasgow, the fifth floor of the Mitchell Library is now an ancestral research hub branded as 'Family History at the Mitchell', which includes Glasgow City Archives, the NHS Greater Glasgow and Clyde Archives, the city's Registrars service (which provides access to the ScotlandsPeople service), and the library's Special Collections section. A gateway site at **www.glasgowfamilyhistory.org.uk** allows you to access guides to all of the facilities, with many topics of interest.

The online databases and holdings page at **www.glasgowfamilyhistory. org.uk/ExploreRecords/Pages/Online-resources.aspx** is of particular interest, with many fascinating databases such as Boer War Burgesses (1900–1904), Glasgow burgh licensed Chimney Sweeps (1852–1862), and a militia registers index (1810–1831). Ancestry has digitised some holdings, such as 'Glasgow, Lanarkshire, Scotland, Electoral Registers, 1857–1962' collection, as sourced from Special Collections, and the 'Glasgow, Scotland, Crew Lists, 1863–1901' database, with information held by the city archive.

An older but equally impressive site is the Virtual Mitchell photographic collection at **www.mitchelllibrary.org/virtualmitchell**, which carries many free-to-view holdings from both the archive and Glasgow Museums. A list of old streets in Glasgow which changed their names before the 1940s is available at **www.glasgowguide.co.uk/info-streetschanged1.html**.

The Glasgow City Archives site at **www.glasgowlife.org.uk/libraries/ city-archives** provides a further wealth of detail on the institution's holdings, with informative guides on collections related to schools, estates, shipbuilding, poor law material, business, police, sasines, church and more. The archive has had many of the city's pre-1995 burial records

*The Mitchell Library, Glasgow.*

digitised in partnership with FamilySearch, with the content available to view at **https://bit.ly/GlasgowCemeteryRecords**.

The collection includes records for the Glasgow Necropolis, the Eastern Necropolis, the Southern Necropolis, the Western Necropolis, Lambhill Cemetery, Cardonald Cemetery, Carmunnock Cemetery, Craigton Cemetery, Eastwood Cemetery, Riddrie Park Cemetery, Sandymount Cemetery, St Kentigern's Catholic Cemetery, and Tollcross Cemetery. At the time of writing the majority were accessible as browse-only digital microfilms, although a small number of rolls had still to be digitised. Cemetery maps for Glasgow are available at **www. glasgowfamilyhistory.org.uk/ExploreRecords/Pages/Burial-Lair-and-Cremation-Registers.aspx**. FindmyPast also hosts a collection entitled 'Scotland, Glasgow & Lanarkshire Death & Burial Index'.

Many monumental inscriptions for Glasgow and Lanarkshire can be found at the Memento Mori site at **www.memento-mori.co.uk**, while a database of interments in the city's Southern Necropolis is available at **https://bit.ly/SouthernNecropolis**. The *Glasgow Evening Times* Roll of Honour index for the First World War is available in PDF format at **www.glasgowfamilyhistory.org.uk/ExploreRecords/Pages/Evening-Times-Roll-of-Honour.aspx**. The city's trade directories, from the 1787 *Nathaniel Jones Directory of Glasgow* to those up to the 1940s at the time of writing, are available on the NLS's Internet Archive portal at **https:// archive.org/details/scottishdirectories**.

Glasgow University Archives Services (**www.gla.ac.uk/myglasgow/ archives/**) has links to both the Scottish Business Archive and the University Archive, with searchable catalogues and guides. The university celebrates its own history at **https://universitystory.gla.ac.uk**, which includes a graduate list (1496–1896) and Rolls of Honour for the two world wars.

Radical Glasgow (**https://bit.ly/RadicalGlasgow**), produced by Caledonian University, has various essays on the insurrections, uprisings and protest movements to have sprung up in the past, from the weavers' strike of 1787 to the foundation of the Scottish Labour Party. The history of Glasgow's hammermen, as recorded by the Scottish Records Society in 1912, can be read at **https://archive.org/details/ historyofhammerm00lums**.

The Glasgow Story (**www.theglasgowstory.com**) has various essays on the city's history, and includes digitised copies of the valuation rolls for 1913–1914, as well as electoral ward maps. For city-based reminiscences, mainly from Bridgeton, visit the Glesga Pals site at **www. glesga.ukpals.com**, where you will find old school photos, a forum and more. To the city's west, Anderston Then and Now (**www.glesga.ukpals. com/profiles/anderston.htm**) recalls the parish's history. Lost Glasgow (**www.lostglasgow.scot**) is a crowdsourcing project which is also seeking to reclaim tales and images from the city's past, and to preserve them.

North Lanarkshire Archives covers Airdrie, Bellshill, Coatbridge, Cumbernauld, Kilsyth, Motherwell, Shotts, Stepps and Wishaw. Its website at **https://culturenl.co.uk/museums/archives-and-local-history-museums/north-lanarkshire-archives/** includes a basic overview of catalogued holdings available in a PDF format download. Additional holdings are catalogued on SCAN (p.8) under archive reference code GB1778. Ancestry has digitised the archive's poor law records for Bothwell, Cambusnethan, Dalziel, New Monkland and Shotts, which are presented as the 'North Lanarkshire, Scotland, Poor Law Applications and Registers, 1849-1917' collection, as well as offering voters records through the 'North Lanarkshire, Scotland, Electoral Registers, 1847–1969' dataset.

A basic introduction to the records at South Lanarkshire Archives, based in East Kilbride, can be read at **www.southlanarkshire.gov.uk/ info/200165/local_and_family_history/588/archives_and_records**. Some additional guides, including histories of Rutherglen, Hamilton palace, and Lanark can be found at **www.southlanarkshire.gov.uk/ info/200165/local_and_family_history**.

Some parish records are available on FreeREG for New Monkland, Old Monkland and Stonehouse.

A Register of Testaments for Hamilton and Campsie (1564–1800), along with Commissariot Records for Glasgow (1547–1800) and Lanark (1595–1800) are available at **www.electricscotland.com/history/records**. The history of the county's mining, ironworks and steel industries can be explored at both **www.sorbie.net/lanarkshire_mining_industry.htm**.

For Airdrie's history visit **www.airdrie.net**, while nearby Monklands is covered at **https://bit.ly/Monklands**, which includes a Lanarkshire parish map and resources on Irish migration to Lanarkshire.

## Midlothian

Until 1921 Midlothian was the County of Edinburgh (Edinburghshire), and as with Glasgow in Lanarkshire, the city of Edinburgh dominates the county and its history. A map of the capital's parish boundaries is available at **www.hoodfamily.info/misc/miscedinmaplarge.html**.

As Scotland's capital city, Edinburgh hosts the National Records of Scotland, the ScotlandsPeople Centre, the National Library of Scotland, Historic Environment Scotland, and the Scottish Catholic Archives, information for which can be found in Chapter 1 and throughout this book.

The Edinburgh City Archives website at **www.edinburgh.gov.uk/ archives/edinburgh-city-archives-1/4** provides downloadable name indexes and subject guides relating to its holdings, as well as information on its Lothians and Borders Police collection. Further items can be located by searching the SCAN catalogue (p.8) and using the archive code GB236.

Ancestry has digitised the archive's voters records for the city of Edinburgh and the burgh of Leith, which are available through its 'Edinburgh, Scotland, Electoral Registers, 1832–1966' collection.

Edinburgh Libraries has a website entitled Our Town Stories site at **www.ourtownstories.co.uk**, where you can explore how the city has evolved across time, and explore some of its many stories. The site connects to a joint project site with Edinburgh Museums and Galleries called Capital Collections (**www.capitalcollections.org.uk**), which depicts images of people and places from the seventeenth century to the present day. This offers the option of finding pictures of Edinburgh by area, date or by browsing a map, as well as through themed exhibitions or via the site's A–Z listing.

The Internet Archive has many digitised Scottish Record Society publications concerning Edinburgh. *A Register of Burials in the Chapel Royal or Abbey of Holyroodhouse 1706–1900* is available at **https://archive.org/ details/scottishrecordso14scotuoft/page/n8**, while marriages from 1564–1800 for Holyroodhouse and Canongate are online at **https://archive.**

*Greyfriars Church, Edinburgh, where the National Covenant was signed in 1638.*

org/details/scottishrecordso34scotuoft/page/n6. Edinburgh marriages from 1595–1700 are presented at https://archive.org/details/register ofmarria33edin/page/n6, and from 1701–1750 at https://archive.org/ details/scottishrecordso23scotuoft. FreeREG has some parish listings for Canongate, Dalry, Edinburgh, Holyrood and Restalrig.

A burial register for the churchyard of Restalrig can also be consulted by visiting https://archive.org/details/scottishrecordso20scotuoft, while the Commissariot Record Edinburgh Registers of Testaments can be found in three volumes at https://archive.org/details/commissariotreco16scot/ page/n6 (1514–1600), https://archive.org/details/scottishrecordso02scot uoft/page/n4 (1601–1700) and https://archive.org/details/scottishrecords o03scotuoft/page/n6 (1701–1800).

Access to these volumes can also be gained via Electric Scotland at www.electricscotland.com/history/records, while the Scots Find site, preserved at https://bit.ly/ScotsFinddatabases, has many of the records presented as downloadable PDF datasets.

For a series of ten short animations depicting the city of Edinburgh from the year 1544, created as part of a University of St Andrew's project entitled *Edinburgh 1544: Virtual Time Binoculars*, visit https://vimeo.com/ search?q=edinburgh%201544.

If your ancestors were Edinburgh-based photographers, you may find more on them at www.edinphoto.org.uk.

FindmyPast has several Edinburgh themed collections:

- Edinburgh Pals 1914–1918
- Scotland, Edinburgh & Lothian Birth and Baptism Index
- Scotland, Edinburgh & Lothian Death and Burial Index
- Scotland, Edinburgh Apprentices 1583–1700
- Scotland, Edinburgh Field Officers From Almanacs 1758–1800
- Scotland, Edinburgh Greyfriars Cemetery Burials 1658–1700
- Scotland, Edinburgh Marriages 1595–1800
- Scotland, Edinburgh St Cuthbert's Census 1790
- Scotland, Edinburgh Temperance Pledges 1886–1908
- Scotland, Fellows of The Royal College of Surgeons of Edinburgh 1581–1873
- Scotland, University Of Edinburgh Graduations 1583–1858

TheGenealogist offers access to *The Edinburgh Academy Register 1824– 1914*.

For the wider county of Midlothian, the county archives site at www. midlothian.gov.uk/info/458/local_and_family_history/30/midlothian_

**archives/2** provides downloadable guides to holdings, with further documents catalogued on SCAN (p.8) under archive code GB 584.

The Lothian Health Services Archives site at **www.lhsa.lib.ed.ac.uk** has a searchable catalogue of holdings for medical matters. The Lothians Family History Society site (**www.lothiansfamilyhistorysociety.co.uk**) has a guide to Midlothian parishes. For the history of coal mining in the county, visit **www.hoodfamily.info/index.html**.

Elsewhere, a one-place study for Corstorphine at **www.angelfire.com/ct2/corstorphine** has directories and the local 1841 census. A similar study for Duddingston at **www.ancestor.abel.co.uk/Duddingston.html** has poll tax testaments, parish records, monumental inscriptions, and other resources. A blog-based site on the history of Leith is at **www.leithhistory. co.uk**, with the town also covered at **www.leithlocalhistorysociety.org. uk** through the Leith Local History Society, which provides a useful timeline.

A host of useful resources for Granton exists at **www.grantonhistory. org**, and for a pictorial history of Niddrie visit **http://niddrie.tripod.com**.

For the Stow Parish Archives, visit **http://stowparisharchive.org.uk**. The surviving 1801 census for Stow is available at **https://stataccscot. edina.ac.uk/static/statacc/dist/manuscript/stowcensus**.

## Moray

Moray is served by the Aberdeen and North East Scotland Family History Society (p.107), while details of Moray Council's Local Heritage Services, based in Elgin, are available at **www.moray.gov.uk/moray_ standard/page_1537.html**.

The service's LIBINDX catalogue at **http://libindx.moray.gov.uk/ mainmenu.asp** includes searchable databases of people, places and subjects contained within the county's archives, with well over 200,000 individuals listed under its People Search alone. Among its holdings are local government archives from the thirteenth century to 1975, local newspapers, gravestone inscriptions, non-established church records to 1855, architectural plans, books, family histories etc. The same collection is accessible as a third-party database on Ancestry, where it is listed as the 'Web: Moray, Scotland, Local Heritage Index, 1632–2014' at **www. ancestry.co.uk/search/collections/70769**.

The Moray Burial Ground Research Group (**www.mbgrg.org**) carries a headstone index, including forename, surname, age and year of death (where known), and in the case of war memorials, regiment. Burial grounds and memorials can be searched individually, and there is a dedicated index for inscriptions found on buried headstones uncovered by the team during its survey work of old cemeteries in the region: the full transcriptions can be sourced from the society's publications. The website also hosts a gallery, a map of the area, a research progress chart and newsletters. A burial index to several Morayshire cemeteries is also available at Highland Memorial Inscriptions at **https://sites.google.com/site/highlandmemorialinscriptions/home**.

The Moray Family History Sharing site at **www.wakefieldfhs.org.uk/morayweb/index.htm** has a message board, databases for the 1851 and 1861 censuses, photographs from the county and several further Moray-based resources.

FindmyPast hosts a database entitled 'Scotland, People of Banffshire & Moray 1150–1857'. While the source for this is not listed, it appears to include material from Bruce Bishop's impressive series of books forming his *The Lands and People of Moray* series, with material drawn from kirk session records, parish records and estate papers. Further details on Bruce's books are available at **www.scottishgenealogicalresearch.co.uk/publications.html**.

A site for Lossiemouth is found at **www.lossiefowk.co.uk** which contains various records and forums, including details from the war memorials and articles on local subjects such as fishing.

Several nineteenth-century editions of Russell's *Morayshire Register* are available on the Internet Archive, while Charles Matheson's *Cambridge County Geography for Moray and Nairn*, published 1915, is available at **https://archive.org/details/moraynairn00math/page/n6**. The Morayshire Roll of Honour can also be found at **https://archive.org/details/morayshirerollof1921mora**.

## Nairnshire

Nairnshire, to the east of Inverness, is covered by several of the same resources focussing on the Highland capital, including Highland Archives and the Highland Family History Society (p.11).

Copies of the *Nairnshire Mirror, and General Advertiser* and *Nairnshire Telegraph and General Advertiser for the Northern Counties* are included within the British Newspaper Archive (p.67). The Am Baile website at **www.ambaile.org.uk** (see Invernessshire) also has many resources for Nairn-based folk, as does the Scottish Highlander Photo Archive at **www.scottishhighlanderphotoarchive.co.uk/genealogists.html**.

A page dedicated to the war memorial in Cawdor is available at **www.spanglefish.com/CWMC**, which includes detailed information on the fallen. Memorial records for some Nairnshire cemeteries can be found indexed at Highland Memorial Inscriptions at **https://sites.google.com/ site/highlandmemorialinscriptions/home**.

Charles Matheson's *Cambridge County Geography for Moray and Nairn*, published 1915, is available at **https://archive.org/details/ moraynairn00math**, while *The Lintie o'Moray: a collection of songs, written for and sung at the anniversary meetings of the Edinburgh Morayshire Society, from 1829 to 1841*, can be accessed at **https://archive.org/details/ lintieomoraycoll00ramp**. J. Watson's *Morayshire Described: Being a Guide to Visitors, Containing Notices of Ecclesiastical and Military Antiquities; Topographical Descriptions of the Principal Country Residences, Towns, and Villages, and Genealogical Notes of the Leading Families in the Country* (1868) is further available at **https://archive.org/details/morayshiredescri00wats**.

For the history of Nairn County Football Club, including players and match statistics gong back to 1919, visit **www.nairncountyarchive.co.uk**.

## Orkney

The Orkney Library and Archive website at **www.orkneylibrary.org.uk** has an online catalogue of resources held at the facility and some resources which members can access from home. The Archive section of the site has a page dedicated to its Local Studies collection, information on the Orkney Sound Archive, its Photographic Archive, some downloadable catalogue resources, and an index to the Orkney register of sea fishing boats from 1852–1968. The facility also has its own dedicated and often humorous blog at **https://orkneyarchive.blogspot.com**.

Sib Folk is the website of the Orkney Family History Society (**https:// orkneyfhs.co.uk**), although at the time of writing many of its resource page links were down. The OrkneyJar project at **www.orkneyjar.com** is packed with resources on the history, folklore, traditions and placenames of the islands, including all sorts of fascinating gems, such as the history of the Orcadian dialect, which has been heavily influenced by the Old Norse language of Norrœna, or 'Norn'.

A parish map is located at **www.genuki.org.uk/big/sct/OKI/indexpars. html**. For historic images of the island, almost 8,000 photographs are hosted at **www.theoldhometown.com**. Further maps, and gravestones from the islands of Rousay, Egilsay, Wyre and Eynhallow, are available at Rousay Roots (**www.rousayroots.com**). The site also hosts censuses for these islands from 1841–1901 (with Eynhallow uninhabited since 1851), and various family histories. For a history of Ness Battery, visit **www. nessbattery.co.uk**.

Orkney Genealogy (**https://bit.ly/cursiter**) hosts an impressive index of baptisms, marriages and deaths, some digitised images from *Ane*

*Account of the Ancient & Present State of Orkney* by the minister of Kirkwall in 1684, and links to useful resources elsewhere. FreeREG has listings for Abune-the-Hill, Birsay, Deerness, Eday, Evie, Firth, Flotta, Harray, Holm and Paplay, Hoy, Hoy and Graemsay, Kirkwall, North Ranaldsay, Orphir, Papa Westray, Rousay, Sandwick, St Andrews, Stenness, Stromness, Stronsay, Walls and Westray.

For South Ronaldsay and Burray visit **www.southronaldsay.net** for resources including a database of the 1821 census, covering the two islands, Swona and the Pentland Skerries. This is also accessible via FindmyPast's 'Scotland, Orkney, 1821 South Ronaldsay & Burray Census' dataset.

Although primarily a Northern Irish website, Eddie's Extracts lists extracts from the Register of Deceased Seamen at **www.eddiesextracts. com/register/index.html**, including extracts for Orkney from 1910–1924

Several nineteenth-century editions of Peace's *Orkney and Shetland Almanac*, and publications from the Orkney Natural History Society, are available on the Internet Archive. Other gems include A.W. Johnston's *Orkney and Shetland folk, 872–1350* (1914) at **https://archive.org/details/ orkneyshetlandfo00john**, and Records of the Earldom of Orkney 1299– 1614 at **https://archive.org/details/recordsofearldom00clou**.

## Peebles-shire

The archives for the Borders county of Peeblesshire (also known as Tweeddale) are held at the Heritage Hub in Hawick (p.116), with the county also served by Borders Family History Society. The society has a dedicated page on the county at **www.bordersfhs.org.uk/p_shire.asp**, which contains an interactive parish map with links to pages containing detailed information on records held within its archive and elsewhere across Scotland.

*A History of Peebleshire* from 1864, by William Chambers, is available at **https://archive.org/details/historyofpeebles00chamiala**. Various directories for the county can be found on the Internet Archive, as well as parish and burgh histories. For *Charters and Documents Relating to the Burgh of Peebles* visit **https://archive.org/details/chartersdocument00peeb**, while *Kirkurd; a Peeblesshire Congregation* can be read at **https://archive. org/details/rschsv06p2couper**. For *Works, Containing the Description of Tweeddale, and Miscellaneous Poems*, visit **https://archive.org/details/ workscontainingd00pennuoft**.

The 1841–1861 censuses from Peeblesshire have been transcribed and made freely available at Scottish Indexes. As with its other border counties holdings, the locations in most entries have links provided to connect them to an online map hosted by the National Library of Scotland, which helpfully allows you to examine the environment where your ancestors lived.

## Perthshire

Perth and Kinross Archive covers both the historic counties of Perthshire and Kinrossshire, and has a gateway platform at **www.culturepk.org. uk/archive-local-family-history**. This provides access to the archive's online catalogue, collection guides, local history films and the following searchable databases:

- Jacobites in Perthshire
- Militia Collection PE66 1680–1891
- Perthshire Militia Petitions 1704–1859 & 1790–1810
- Perthshire Militia Certifications 1802–1810
- Assorted Perthshire Militia Papers 1680–1891 & 1785–1820
- Perth burgh burial registers, 1794–1855
- Perthshire People & Kinross-shire Kin
- Railway Sources
- Threiplands' People
- World War One Sources
- World War One Newspapers
- World War Two Sources

The Friends of the Archives section also carries newsletters from the year 2000 onwards, with various interesting features.

The archive's burial registers collection is available on Ancestry as a third-party database, entitled Web: Perth, Scotland, Burgh Burial Index, 1794–1855. Ancestry also has several additional Perth and Perthshire-based collections sourced from the archive, as follows:

- Perth and Kinross, Scotland, Electoral Registers, 1832–1961
- Perthshire, Scotland, Cess, Stent and Valuation Rolls, 1650–1899
- Perth, Scotland, Survey of Inhabitants, 1766, 1773
- Perth, Scotland, Register of Deeds, 1566–1811
- Perthshire, Scotland, School Registers of Admission and Withdrawals, 1869–1902
- Perthshire, Scotland, Militia Survey, 1802
- Perth, Scotland Newspaper Index Cards, 1809–1990

FindmyPast also hosts 'Scotland, Perthshire, Inhabitants of the Burgh of Perth 1766', as sourced from the Scottish Genealogy Society.

The website of the Friends of the Dundee City Archives group has uploaded details of Perthshire vehicle registrations (1909–1911) within the Transport records section of the site at **www.fdca.org.uk**. Other county-wide resources for Perthshire include **www.perthshire-scotland.co.uk/towns.htm**, which hosts brief histories for main towns in the county, and the Perthshire Diary site (**www.perthshirediary.com**), which recalls 365 moments in the history of the county arranged as a daily digest.

Tay Valley Family History Society (p.110), covers the whole of Perthshire. A separate society, North Perthshire Family History Group, folded in 2018, but the data that was formerly hosted on its website is now included on the site of the Pitlochry and Moulin Heritage Centre at **www.pitlochryandmoulinheritagecentre.co.uk/genealogy.html**, and includes census, death and burial records, as well as a parish map for North Perthshire. For Pitlochry itself, the Pitlochry Down Memory Lane Facebook is available at **www.facebook.com/Pitlochry-down-memory-lane-413632115379322**.

The Glenlyon History Society (Comann Eachdraidh Ghleann Lìomhann) has several old photos and Rena Stewart's Glenlyon Memories recollections available at **www.glenlyon.org**.

A plan of the burgh of Perth from the early 1800s is at **https://bit.ly/burghmapofPerth1800s**. The former Alternative Perth site has been preserved at **https://bit.ly/AlternativePerth** and holds a virtual encyclopaedia of material related to the burgh of Perth (and Perthshire), with many biographies of important folk and gazetteer entries. Transcriptions of records from the Weavers Incorporation of Perth, including the names of apprentices, journeymen bookings, incorporation minutes, weavers bearing arms in 1715, a list of weavers paying for seats in St. John's Kirk in 1749, and weavers listed in King James VI Hospital rentals and chartularies from 1628–1816 have been transcribed and made available at **https://scotlandsgreateststory.wordpress.com/free-items**. Also available are transcripts of *Memorabilia of the City of Perth* (1806) and my university dissertation, *The Role of King James VI Hospital in Perth as a 19th century feudal superior*.

Papers in a Trunk (**www.highlandstrathearn.com**) is another encyclopaedic project carrying essays on the history of Strathearn, with its associated clans and families. Many electoral rolls for the county from 1832 can be found at **https://caledonianconnectionsgenealogy.blogspot.com**.

*The author's grandfather, David Hepburn Paton, was born in Blackford in 1864.*

FreeREG has records for Callander and Kilmadock. For Blackford's history, visit **www.blackfordhistoricalsociety.org.uk**, while Dunning Parish Historical Society has a monumental inscriptions index at **www.dunning.uk.net**, and census entries from 1841–1891. Inscriptions for Dunblane are recorded at **www.memento-mori. co.uk**, with the history of the town itself recorded at **www.dunblaneweb.co.uk**. For Forgandenny, the original responses for the First Statistical Account in the 1790s, as recorded by Robert Thomas, can be read at **https://stataccscot.edina. ac.uk/static/statacc/dist/manuscript/ forgandennyms**.

The Library of Innerpeffray holds a borrowers' register noting people from 1747–1968 who have used the facility. Visit **www.innerpeffraylibrary.co.uk/borrowers-register.php** to download Jill Dye's dissertation on the subject, which includes a spreadsheet listing the names of all borrowers and details of the books they borrowed.

### Renfrewshire

Renfrewshire is today administered by both Renfrewshire Council and East Renfrewshire Council.

The Renfrewshire Libraries site at **https://libcat.renfrewshire.gov.uk/ iguana/www.main.cls** provides information under its Heritage tab on Family History, Local History, and the Heritage Centre in Paisley. Through these you will find various guides to resources held at the Paisley-based centre, including a dedicated page on Paisley's poor law records, with a downloadable index for the period from 1839–1948, at **https://libcat. renfrewshire.gov.uk/iguana/www.main.cls?surl=PoorLaw**. An index to *The Paisley Advertiser* and *The Renfrewshire Advertiser* from 1824–1883 is also available at **https://libcat.renfrewshire.gov.uk/iguana/uploads/ file/Newspaper%20Index%201824-1883.pdf**. FindmyPast further hosts a 'Scotland, Renfrewshire, Paisley Poll Tax 1695 database'.

East Renfrewshire Archives (**www.eastrenfrewshire.gov.uk/archives**) hosts a searchable catalogue for its holdings in Clarkston, as well as downloadable subject guides. The council's Portal to the Past site at **www.portaltothepast.co.uk** includes a detailed family history section and hosts online exhibitions such as a history of the region in the First World War, Great Scottish Minds and Innovations, and more focussed essays such as the history of Shanks & Co. brass foundry. The site also includes a catalogue of the council's archival holdings.

Information about Renfrewshire Family History Society, including a journal index, can be found at **http://renfrewshirefhs.co.uk**, while the Renfrewshire Local History Forum at **https://rlhf.info** promotes all aspects of history and archaeology in both Renfrewshire and Inverclyde. Glasgow and West of Scotland Family History Society also covers the area (p.131).

The Greenock-based Watt Library has a family history page at **www.inverclyde.gov.uk/community-life-and-leisure/heritage-services/watt-library**, with various downloadable resources, while its Local History page at **www.inverclyde.gov.uk/community-life-and-leisure/heritage-services/watt-library/local-history** is absolutely packed with digitised resources, including photographs, directories, and its extensive newspaper indexes.

A register of marriages and baptisms from the parish of Kilbarchan (1649–1772) is online at **https://archive.org/details/scottishrecordso41 scotuoft**. FreeREG also has coverage for Kilbarchan.

For Daniel Weir's *History of the Town of Greenock* (1829), visit **https://books.google.co.uk/books?id=8qQHAAAAQAAJ**.

Ancestry hosts three books for the county, which can be searched or browsed: *A History of the County of Renfrew From the Earliest Times* (1905), *The History of the Shire of Renfrew* (1782), and *Archaeological and Historical Collections Relating to the County of Renfrew Parish of Lochwinnoch* (1885–1890).

## Ross and Cromarty

The historic counties of Rossshire and Cromartyshire are today part of the Highland Council area, and are served by Highland Archives in Inverness (p.126).

Ross and Cromarty Heritage Society hosts various resources for many communities within the county at **www.rossandcromartyheritage.org**, including war memorials, parish records, an interactive map, and more. Ross and Cromarty Roots (**www.rosscromartyroots.co.uk**) is equally useful with contextual essays on subjects such as the Church, schools, the poor, farming and the Clearances, while also providing some graveyard location information.

Highland Family History Society (p.111) includes resources for the region, while many of the county's folk are included in the Scottish

Highlander Photo Archive (**www.scottishhighlanderphotoarchive. co.uk**). An index to the monumental inscriptions to some sixty-seven cemeteries and kirkyards in Ross and Cromarty can be found at Highland Memorial Inscriptions at **https://sites.google.com/site/ highlandmemorialinscriptions/home**.

Am Baile (p.127) also covers the county, with one of its most impressive holdings being a 44-page downloadable book on *The Cromarty Fisherfolk Dialect* (locate this through the main Search box). For a general guide to the main towns and villages in the Black Isle visit **www.black-isle.info**.

An 1814 militia list for males aged between seventeen and forty-five is available for the royal burgh of Cromarty at **https://bit.ly/ CromartyMilitia**, while a list of householders from 1744 is at **https://bit. ly/Cromarty1744**. A history of Kirkmichael and the Urquhart clan in the Black Isle is at **www.kirkmichael.info**.

Old photos of the region are available at **www.theoldhometown. com**, while a site on the history of the parish of Resolis is located at **https://bit.ly/Resolis**. For the Coigach in the east of the county, there are considerable resources located at **https://freepages.rootsweb. com/~coigach/genealogy/index.htm**, including militia lists, gazetteer entries, emigration records, census records, and a 1775 map showing the locations of farms in the region.

FreeREG has records for Aird, Bac, Branahuie, Col, Contin, Garrabost, Habost, Holm, Knock, Lochs, Melbost, Pabail, Steinish, Stornoway, Tolsta, Tong, Uig and Vatisker.

The Fearn Peninsula Graveyards Project database (**www. fearnpeninsulagraveyards.com**) is another excellent resource with nearly 7,000 memorials. For the heritage centre at Applecross, an online catalogue is hosted at **www.applecrossheritage.org.uk**, along with a brief history of the area.

A *Ross-shire Roll of Honour, with Souter's Ross-shire Directory* from 1915, including portraits of officers and men on active service, is available at **https://archive.org/details/rossshirerollofh1915sout**, while *The Days of the Fathers in Ross-shire* (1867) looks at the history of the church and ministers in the county at **https://archive.org/details/thedaysofthefath00kennuoft**.

Biographically, *Rossiana; Papers and Documents Relating to the History and Genealogy of the Ancient and Noble House of Ross, of Ross-shire* (1908) is available at **https://archive.org/details/rossianapapersdo01read**, while *The Families of Gordon of Invergordon, Newhall, also Ardoch, Ross-shire, and Carroll, Sutherland* (1906) is available at **https://archive.org/details/ familiesofgordon00bull**.

For *Old Ross-shire and Scotland, as Seen in the Tain and Balnagown Documents*, visit **https://archive.org/details/oldrossshirescot00macguoft/page/n12**, and to browse *The Gaelic Psalm tunes of Ross-shire and the Neighbouring Counties*, visit **https://archive.org/details/gaelicpsalmtunes00edin**.

## Roxburghshire

The main archive in the former county of Roxburghshire is the Heritage Hub at Hawick (p.116). The Borders Family History Society has a web page for Roxburghshire at **www.bordersfhs.org.uk/r_shire.asp**, which includes an interactive parish map, while elsewhere the site also hosts a poor law records database for Jedburgh and a discussion forum.

FreeREG has coverage for Bowden, Castleton, Cavers, Crailing, Melrose, Roxburgh, Smailholm, Southdean, Sprouston and St Boswells. The 1841–1861 censuses have been transcribed and made freely available at ScottishIndexes, while several other generic websites on the Borders include material from Roxburghshire (see Berwickshire, p.116).

Melrose Parish Registers (1642–1840), compiled by the Scottish Record Society in 1913, can be viewed at **www.archive.org/details/scottishrecordso33scotuoft**. For the history of Denholm, its quarrying industry, church history, stocking industry and more, see **www.denholmvillage.co.uk**.

The History of Kelso (**https://bit.ly/historyofkelso**) records the story of the town from 1113 to the First World War, while FindmyPast hosts a 'Roxburghshire, Kelso Dispensary Patient Registers 1777–1781' collection. For Maxton, visit **https://bit.ly/maxtonscotland** to view the history section and some black and white images. The history of Jedburgh is at **www.jedburgh.org.uk**.

Four volumes of the *History and Antiquities of Roxburghshire and Adjacent Counties* (1855–1864) are available on the Internet Archive. *Border Memories, or Sketches of Prominent Men and Women of the Border* (1876) is at **https://archive.org/details/bordermemorieso00taitgoog**, while the *Memoir of the Late Rev. John Baird, Minister of Yetholm, Roxburghshire, with an Account of His Labours in Reforming the Gipsy Population of that Parish* (1862) is at **https://archive.org/details/memoirlaterevjo00bairgoog**.

## Selkirkshire

As with Roxburghshire, Selkirkshire is catered for by the Hawick Heritage Hub (p.116), while Borders Family History Society has a page for Selkirkshire at **www.bordersfhs.org.uk/s_shire.asp**, which includes a parish map.

The History of Selkirk (**https://bit.ly/HistoryofSelkirk**) provides introductory essays on various subjects of interest, including the Covenanters, the Reivers, Selkirk Abbey and the history of the Selkirk Common Riding.

For a list of Selkirk burgh inhabitants on 16 June 1817 visit **www.cangenealogy.com/armstrong/selkirk1817.htm**. Selkirk Antiquarian Society's pages at **www.selkirkshireantiquariansociety.co.uk** contain lists of deaths and monumental inscriptions records, which can be purchased. Transcriptions of statutory death records from the county in 1874 can also be viewed at **https://freepages.rootsweb.com/~connochie/genealogy/bdm/seldeaths1874.html**, while census records from 1841–1861 are freely available at Scottish Indexes.

## Shetland

Shetland Museum and Archives (**www.shetlandmuseumandarchives.org.uk**) provides an online summary of local history holdings, and its fully searchable photo collection is available at **https://photos.shetlandmuseumandarchives.org.uk**. Shetland Library's Local Collection page at **www.shetland-library.gov.uk/Localcollection.asp** includes information on researching family history within the islands.

The islands' heritage is explored at both **www.shetland-heritage.co.uk**, and **www.shetlandheritageassociation.com**, while Shetland Family History Society (**www.shetland-fhs.org.uk**) offers a map showing various parishes across the islands.

A free database of names from across the islands, sourced from many different records, is the North Isles Family History project at **www.bayanne.info/Shetland**, while a Shetland DNA project is hosted at **www.davidkfaux.org/shetlandislandsY-DNA.html**. FreeREG has records for Foula, Papa Stour, Sandness and Walls.

The Scalloway Museum website at **www.scallowaymuseum.org** provides information on local people and events. Among the topics covered are the village's industrial heritage and wartime experience, including the Second World War 'Shetland Bus' to occupied Norway.

Transcripts of the 1841, 1851, 1861, 1871 and 1891 censuses for the Isle of Foula are available at **https://bit.ly/Foulacensuses**. For the parish of Tingwall, FindmyPast hosts 'Scotland, Shetland, Tingwall List of Inhabitants 1785'.

Janice Halcrow's Shetland newspaper transcriptions, including all BMD intimations from the *Shetland Times* from 1872–1990, are available on FindmyPast. Further intimations from the same paper from 1930–1988 can also be accessed at **www.users.on.net/~bruce.smith**.

*The County Families of the Shetland Islands, Being Genealogies of Local Families Compiled from Public Records and Other Sources* (1893) is accessible at **https://archive.org/details/TheCountyFamiliesOfTheShetlandIslands**. For *Shetland Folk-lore* (1899), visit **https://archive.org/details/shetland folklor00spengoog**.

## Stirlingshire

Stirling Archives (**www.stirling.gov.uk/archives**) hosts an online catalogue and basic information on how to access its holdings. On a parallel blog site at **www.stirlingarchives.scot**, the archive also offers poor relief indexes for much of the county. The county library service has its own catalogue available via **www.stirling.gov.uk/libraries-archives**. Central Scotland Family History Society (**www.csfhs.org.uk**) is the main family history group for the area.

Transcriptions of statutory deaths in Stirlingshire in 1869 can be found at **https://freepages.rootsweb.com/~connochie/genealogy/bdm/stideaths1869.html**, while many monumental indexes for burial grounds across the county can be found at **www.memento-mori.co.uk**. For the history of Stirling town, and descriptions of several heritage sites, visit **www.stirling.co.uk**.

The history of the Holy Trinity Scottish Episcopal Church in Stirling is available at **www.holytrinitystirling.org/ourbuilding.htm**, and includes the roll of honour for the Argyll and Sutherland Highlanders, with which the church has had a long association. A separate index also details those named on memorials within the church.

The University of Strathclyde's Bannockburn Genetic Genealogy Project is available at **www.strathgenealogy.org.uk/projects/bannockburn-genetic-genealogy-project**, along with additional information on some of the battle's participants at **www.strathgenealogy.org.uk/bannockburn**.

The Drymen Millennium Project (**www.drymen-history.org.uk/millennium.html**) has a useful list of publications on Drymen's history, while the Milngavie Online project (**www.milngavieonline.com/about**) has some history resources including a list of estates. For Killearn visit **https://killearnontheweb.co.uk**.

The history of Kilsyth is explored at **http://kilsyth.org.uk**, with some monumental inscriptions for the town available at **http://members.tripod.com/~Caryl_Williams/Kilsyth-7.html**, and a handful of transcribed OPR records from 1737, 1741, 1748 and 1762 further available at **http://members.iinet.net.au/~kjstew/KilsythOPRS.htm**. Visit **https://falkirklocalhistory.club** for a detailed overview of Falkirk, including a photo album and detailed articles on aspects of the local history. FreeREG has records for Kippen.

The Internet Archive hosts two volumes of William Nimmo's *History of Stirlingshire* (1880), as well as *The Placename of Stirlingshire* at **https://archive.org/details/placenamesofstir00johnuoft**. A *Report on the Housing of Miners in Stirlingshire and Dumbartonshire* (1911) is at **https://archive.org/details/b21366329**.

## Sutherland

The northern county of Sutherland is catered for by Highland Archives (p.126), and the Highland Family History Society (p.111).

The County Sutherland site at **https://cosuthfamhistory.blogspot.com** contains an excellent guide to the region's communities, while the Burial Grounds of Sutherland site at **https://public.fotki.com/rhemusaig/burial_grounds** provides images from various graveyards, as well as information on the churches and areas within which they are based. For names on the war memorials of Sutherland visit **https://cosuthtribute.blogspot.com**. The Highland Memorial Inscriptions site (**https://sites.google.com/site/highlandmemorialinscriptions/home**) has an index to some twenty-six burial sites within the county.

The Sutherland Papers (**www.sutherlandcollection.org.uk**) is an online platform hosting archive material of the Leveson-Gower family, Marquesses of Stafford and Dukes of Sutherland. Although primarily concerned with their English holdings, the site does also cover Sutherland to a limited extent. For the story of the family's involvement in the Sutherland Clearances visit **https://en.wikipedia.org/wiki/Highland_Clearances**.

The Glencalvie Clearance and Croick Church at **www.scotshistory.jejik.co.uk/croick/croick.html** further recalls the Clearances from the area in 1845, while the Kildonan Clearance is recalled at **http://glendiscovery.com/kildonan-clearance.html**. A community site for Helmsdale at **www.helmsdale.org** includes various history essays on subjects as diverse as local football, the police, the Clearances and emigration.

The Dornoch-based Historylinks Museum (**www.historylinks.org.uk**) hosts a local history section, which includes biographies of famous locals, as well as a roll of honour and information from the area's war graves. The history of Brora is included at **www.broratek.co.uk/broraweb/family-tree.html**, with Golspie catered for at **www.spanglefish.com/golspieheritagesociety**. The story of the mills in Golspie is explored at **www.golspiemill.co.uk/mill/history.html**, while the folklore of the area is further covered at **www.archive.org/stream/ golspiecontribut00nich#page/n6/mode/2up**.

FreeREG has records for Assynt and Eddrachillis, while the Internet Archive hosts a digitised facsimile at **https://archive.org/details/ scottishrecordso26scotuoft** of a Scottish Records Society publication from 1911 containing the parish register of Durness (1764–1814). *A Tour in Sutherlandshire, with Extracts from the Fieldbooks of a Sportsman and Naturalist*, by Charles St John (1849), is at **https://archive.org/details/ tourinsutherland01stjorich**.

## West Lothian

West Lothian was known as Linlithgowshire until 1921. The council's History and heritage site at **www.westlothian.gov.uk/history-and-heritage** has various historical resources as well as details of the council's archival holdings, held in Livingston. The Family History section lists holdings at West Lothian Local History Library, with access also to its newspaper index at **https://wlcls.ent.sirsidynix.net.uk/client/en_GB/ newsindex/**.

West Lothian Family History Society (**www.wlfhs.org.uk**) has several resources available, including transcriptions from war memorials across the county (and images from the Scottish Korean War Memorial), a parish list, a picture gallery and a History of West Lothian, as well as a discussion forum. Lothians Family History Society (**www. lothiansfamilyhistorysociety.co.uk**) includes a list of parishes across West Lothian, and hosts a Facebook page at **www.facebook.com/people/ Lothians-Fhs/100009903970976**.

FindmyPast has the following databases for the county:

- Scotland, Linlithgowshire (West Lothian), Electoral Registers 1864–1931
- Scotland, Linlithgowshire (West Lothian), Poorhouse Records 1859–1912

For indexes to monumental inscriptions at Bo'ness, Carriden and Linlithgow visit Memento Mori (**www.memento-mori.co.uk**). The West Lothian Gravestone Photographic Resource Project has various burial sites from the county indexed at **www.gravestonephotos.com/public/ area.php?area=West%20Lothian**, namely for Dalmeny, West Calder, Kirkliston, and South Queensferry, with others on the way.

A one-place study for Armadale is available at **www.armadale.org.uk/ indexhistory.htm**, with historic maps and more. A site on Broxburn and

Uphall is also available at **www.broxburnanduphall.com**, containing the 1841 and 1851 censuses, monumental inscriptions from St Nicholas Kirk, war memorials, and essays on life in the village's past. FreeREG has listing for Bo'ness and Torphichen.

The *Cambridge County Geography for Linlithgowshire* (1912) is at **https://archive.org/details/linlithgowshire00muiruoft**, while *The Poets and Poetry of Linlithgowshire* (1896) is available at **https://archive.org/details/poetspoetryoflin00biss**. For *The Binns: Charter Granted on Ninth November, 1944 to the National Trust for Scotland by Eleanor Dalyell of The Binns*, visit **https://archive.org/details/binnschartergran00nati**.

## Wigtownshire

Wigtownshire is served by Dumfries and Galloway Archive (p.120), and the 1851 census for the county, and shipping registers for Wigtown (1836–1908), can be consulted on its site at **https://info.dumgal.gov.uk/HistoricalIndexes**.

The Wigtownshire Pages at **http://freepages.history.rootsweb.ancestry.com/~leighann/index.html** include separate vital records indexes from both parish registers and the *Wigtownshire Free Press* (starting in 1843), a parish map, death registers transcriptions, commissariat records of Wigtown Testaments (1700–1800) and much more.

*Portpatrick harbour, where many Irish couples historically arrived on day trips to avail themselves of Scotland's laws on irregular marriage.*

A 1912 trade directory for the town is available at **https://homepages. rootsweb.com/~scottish/TradeDirectory1912.html**, while Dumfries and Galloway Family History Society (**https://dgfhs.org.uk**) has a map of the area from 1862.

The website of the Stranraer and District Local History Trust at **www. stranraerhistory.org.uk** also contains lists of recordings in its audio archive and its books on the history of the county. For the history of Portpatrick and its kirk, as well as an interactive map with details on the graveyard burials, and the story of shipwrecks in the area, visit **www. portpatrickchurchyard.org.uk**.

*The Parish Lists of Wightownshire and Minnigaff 1684* (1916) can be read at **https://archive.org/details/parishlistsofwig72scot**. The information from this book is also available on FindmyPast in a database entitled 'Scotland, Wigtownshire & Minnigaff Parish Lists 1684'. Ancestry also hosts two databases for the county – 'Charter Chest of the Earldom of Wigtown, 1214–1681' and 'Wigtown, Scotland Charter Chest, 1214–1681'

## The Western Isles

The Western Isles (Na h-Eileanan an Iar) never formed a single county historically, and have been divided between Invernessshire, Ross and Cromarty, and Argyll. While some resources have been listed in the county holdings above, the following sources may also be of some further assistance.

Hebridean Connections (**www.hebrideanconnections.com**) provides resources for many *comainn eachdraidh* (historical societies) from the

*The Hebridean Connections page provides links to various* comainn eachdraidh *across the Western Isles.*

Outer Hebrides. Records can be searched for through an interactive map or by browsing datasets. Among the superb holdings is a list of crofts and their past residents.

Hebridean Archives/Tasglann nan Eilean Siar (**www.tasglann.org. uk/en**) provides a range of records, and has a catalogue at **http://ica-atom.tasglann.org.uk**. School logbooks for both St Kilda and Mingulay, both of which have now been depopulated, are digitised and available at **www.tasglann.org.uk/en/collections/tasglann-held-archives/schools-records**. Information for school boards and education committee records on other islands is included on the page.

On Lewis, Comann Eachdraidh Uig has a site at **www.ceuig.co.uk** with various historical resources. Among its gems is a map of the island, depicting place names in Old Norse, at **www.ceuig.co.uk/uig-in-old-norse**. Comainn Eachdraidh Pairc has its own site at **www.cepairc.com** with information on its townships and photographs, and the Angus MacLeod Archive (**www.angusmacleodarchive.org.uk**). For the west of Lewis, and for the island of St Kilda, visit the Comann Eachdraidh an Taobh Siar site at **www.ceats.org.uk/archive.htm**.

Graveyards at Dalmore, Kirvick, Sandwick, Stornoway (St Peter's Church), Ness Light House and Rodel (St Callan's) on the Isle of Lewis have been recorded and indexed on the Highland Monumental Inscriptions site (**https://sites.google.com/site/highlandmemorialinscriptions/home**).

Elsewhere on Lewis, visit **www.barvasandbrue.co.uk** for a 1718 Judicial Rental roll of Nether Barvas, a Barvas School logbook from 1899, and an index to articles and photographs in *Fios a'Bhaile*, the newsletter of Comann Eachdraidh Bharabhais agus Bhru. Further resources for Ness to the north of the island are to be found at **www.cenonline.org**. If your ancestors were from North Tosta, the local historical society's site (**www. tolsta.info**) has lists of emigrants, famous folk, galleries and a timeline.

South of Lewis is Harris, and the Seallam! Visitor Centre (**www. hebridespeople.com/visitor-centre**) has details of holdings for the island's family history centre, as run by Bill Lawson's Co Leis Thu? Service (meaning 'Who do you belong to?). The facility also operates the subscription-based Hebrides People (**www.hebridespeople.com**), which includes an emigrants' database. The site has almost 100,000 records for former inhabitants of the parishes of Barvas, Harris, Point, Lochs, Stornoway and Uig.

For the history of Barra, Vatersay, Mingulay, Berneray, Pabbay and Sanday visit **www.barraheritage.com**. Historic images of Berneray are accessible through **www.isleofberneray.com**; for Benbecula visit **www. benbeculahistorysociety.co.uk**.

The holdings of the Clan Donald Centre at Armadale on Skye are explained at **www.armadalecastle.com**, while Sleat Local History Society's site (**www.sleatlocalhistorysociety.org.uk**) has a Gaelic local place name index, old photographs and the histories of various townships. Inscriptions from some graves at Struan's municipal cemetery on the island are at **www.gravestonephotos.com/public/ cemetery.php?cemetery=232&limit=1**. Resources for Elgol and Torrin held by the local historical society are briefly noted at **https:// elgolandtorrinhistoricalsociety.wordpress.com**.

The Isle of Eigg outlines its history at **www.isleofeigg.net**, while for Colonsay and Oronsay visit **www.colonsay.info** to find various census extracts, gravestones inscriptions and nineteenth-century parish records. Resources for Coll can be found at **www.collgenealogy.com**, including the censuses, a map, various vital records, lists of emigrant ships and their passengers and old newspaper articles. A similar site for Tiree at **www.tireegenealogy.com** includes overseas cemetery records and material from the Napier Commission into crofting, while the history of Muck is explored at **www.islemuck.com/geneal.htm**, accompanied by census transcriptions from 1841–1891.

Mull Genealogy (**www.mullgenealogy.co.uk**) has baptism and burial indexes, and a census database covering 1841–1911. There is also a look-up service in the Resources section of the site for books held privately, and some further databases such as rental rolls for the

*The Dun Carloway broch on the Isle of Lewis.*

Torloisk estate and deaths in Kilninian. A list of Mull natives who settled in Prince Edward Island, Canada, is online at **www.islandregister.com/mullnatives.html**. The history of the island of Lismore is explored at **www.lismoregaelicheritagecentre.org**, while historic images of people from the island can be viewed at **www.isleoflismore.com**.

Parish records for Bowmore, Killarow and Kildalton on the island of Islay are online at **https://homepages.rootsweb.ancestry.com/~steve/islay/opr**. A blog-based site for the history of Jura is at **https://isleofjura.scot**. For the history of Gigha and its MacNeill lairds visit **www.gigha.org.uk**.

A *Description of the Western Isles of Scotland, Called Hybrides* (1884) is available at **https://archive.org/details/descriptionwest00monrgoog**, while the second volume of *Origines Parochiales Scotiae: the Antiquities Ecclesiastical and Territorial of the Parishes of Scotland* includes the origins of parishes within the Diocese of the Isles, at **https://archive.org/details/originesparochia00bann**.

*Chapter 6*

# SCOTLAND'S DIASPORA

Scots have helped to define much of the world as it is today, following centuries of emigration, both prior to its partnership with England and Wales to form Britain, and through the shared enterprise that became the British Empire.

The NLS has a site at **https://digital.nls.uk/emigration/resources/** providing many links for the Scots Abroad, while its Emigration from Scotland: Emigrants' Correspondence database at **www.nls.uk/ catalogues/online/scots-abroad/mss** provides a handy bibliography of letters and papers from the library's manuscripts collections, dating from 1685, but mostly from the nineteenth and twentieth century. Professor Tanja Bueltmann's Scottish Diaspora Blog at **http://thescottishdiaspora. net** is another informative site well worth following for interesting posts on the history of Scottish migration and the Scots abroad.

For more recent emigration from the UK, Ancestry hosts 'UK, Outward Passenger Lists, 1890–1960', as sourced from TNA (BT27). The same records are on FindmyPast as the 'Passenger Lists Leaving UK 1890–1960' collection, and on TheGenealogist as part of its 'Passenger Lists' database. FindmyPast also hosts a useful collection entitled 'Index To Register Of Passport Applications 1851–1903', which lists many Scots who sought a passport for travel overseas, although such documents were not compulsory until 1914. Additional passenger lists are available on all the platforms, as well as on FamilySearch.

The following sections detail some of the resources from overseas countries which may also help with your research.

## Ireland
While thousands of Scots today live within the rest of Britain, historically the area of the UK most greatly affected by settlement from Scotland has

undoubtedly been the province of Ulster in Ireland. Many Scots were encouraged to settle in counties Antrim and Down during the Hamilton and Montgomery settlements of 1606, with their story explored at **https:// bit.ly/HamiltonMontgomery1606**. These were followed shortly after by James VI's Plantations of Ulster, with further colonisation by Scots (and English settlers) in counties Armagh, Coleraine (later expanded and renamed Londonderry), Cavan, Donegal, Fermanagh and Tyrone. Many of the immediate descendants of these immigrants later emigrated to the American colonies as the 'Scotch-Irish' because of religious persecution by the Anglican regime in Ireland (p.159).

The Scots brought their Presbyterian religion to Ireland, with the first presbytery established in Carrickfergus in 1642 by a Scottish Covenanting army which invaded during the Wars of the Three Kingdoms; Presbyterianism remains the largest Protestant denomination in Northern Ireland today. They also brought the Scots language (p.27), which is today referred to in Ulster as 'Ulster Scots', 'Lallans', the Scots word for 'lowlands', or by the hybrid term 'Ullans' (Ulster Lallans). A background resource for the language is available at **www.ulsterscotsagency.com/ what-is-ulster-scots/language**, while a specific dictionary for Ulster Scots can be found online at **www.ulsterscotsacademy.com/words/ dictionary/index.php**.

FindmyPast hosts sixty-eight maps detailing settlements during the Plantations of Ulster, and earlier colonisation schemes, as sourced from the State Papers at TNA, and presented within its 'Ireland, Maps and Surveys 1558–1610 Image Browse' set.

*The Hamilton Montgomery Settlement 1606 site has been preserved on the Internet Archive.*

For further resources on researching the descendants of the Scots in Ireland, consult my book *Tracing Your Irish Family History on the Internet (Second Edition)* (p.168).

## England and the British Empire

The British Empire was first founded in the latter sixteenth century and reached its zenith towards the end of the nineteenth century, before ending in the mid-twentieth century. Following the collapse of Scotland's Darien Scheme, and the Union with England and Wales of 1707, the country soon played its part in the creation and administration of the new British Empire, which was already under way with the American colonies. For an overview of the Empire's successes and failings, visit **www.britishempire.co.uk**.

The Royal Commonwealth Society has a massive library of resources for both the Empire and the Commonwealth, with its collection held by Cambridge University. Its online catalogue at **www.lib.cam.ac.uk/rcs** details over 300,000 holdings, including books, pamphlets, periodicals, official publications, manuscripts and photographs, with an online exhibition also available at **www.cam.ac.uk/royalcommonwealthsocietyexhib**. TNA further provides a detailed guide to the empire at **www.nationalarchives.gov.uk/education**, and holds the Foreign and Commonwealth Office's Migrated Records collections (see **https://bit.ly/MigratedArchives**).

One of the Empire's darkest legacies was the transatlantic slave trade, and Scotland was every bit as culpable in this practice as her British partners. The NRS provides an excellent overview of records relating to the trade within its collections, as well as in other repositories, at **www.nrscotland.gov.uk/research/guides/slavery-and-the-slave-trade**. The University of Glasgow made the news in 2019 when it announced that it would be the first UK-based university to pay reparations for the benefits that it derived from the trade. Its Slavery Studies / Eòlas na Tràillealachd platform at **www.gla.ac.uk/schools/humanities/slavery/** details current research projects, while its Runaway Slaves in Eighteenth Century Britain project at **www.runaways.gla.ac.uk** includes examples from Scotland. Many Scots who profited from the slave trade can be identified from University College London's Legacies of British Slave-Ownership site at **www.ucl.ac.uk/lbs**.

Resources for pursuing Scots who moved to England and Wales are discussed in Chapters 1 and 3, but my book *Tracing Your Family History on the Internet (Second Edition)* may assist further (p.168).

*Many Scots who benefited from the slave trade can be identified from the Legacies of British Slave-Ownership website.*

## Europe

For an overview of Scottish migration to mainland Europe, notably to the Netherlands, Russia, Poland and Italy, visit **https://en.wikipedia.org/ wiki/Scottish_people#Scots_in_mainland_Europe**. Further background on Russians claiming Scots ancestry can be found at **https://en.wikipedia. org/wiki/Scottish_Russians**.

Ancestry hosts a David Dobson book entitled *Scots in Poland, Russia and the Baltic States, 1550–1850* in database and browse format at **www. ancestry.co.uk/search/collections/49342**.

## USA

In addition to the early Scottish settlers who travelled to America for a new life were thousands of Scottish prisoners of war, who were deported from Scotland during the seventeenth-century Wars of the Three Kingdoms as indentured servants to the Caribbean and the American colonies, particularly Virginia. In later years Covenanters and Jacobites were similarly transported.

From the early 1700s they were to be joined by many 'Ulster Scots' or 'Scotch-Irish', descendants of seventeenth-century Scottish settlers in the north of Ireland, who were forced to move on following the implementation of the Irish Penal laws against Presbyterians and Roman Catholics. In the Revolutionary War, George Washington noted that 'If defeated elsewhere then I will make my final stand for liberty with the Scotch-Irish of my native Virginia', with others proclaiming the revolution to be a Scotch-Irish Presbyterian rebellion. This hides a somewhat more complicated picture, however, with many soldiers of the British Army also being Scots who were fiercely loyal to the Crown, among them many drawn from the Highlands just a generation after the Jacobite campaigns were finally ended by the carnage of Culloden.

Following the Highland Clearances (p.128) and the agricultural revolution, emigration from Scotland across the Atlantic dramatically increased. An overview of the Scots' history in the US is available at **https://en.wikipedia.org/wiki/Scottish_Americans**.

A database of US-bound indentured servants is available at **www.pricegen.com/immigrantservants/login/login.php**, listing indentures for servants and transported convicts between 1607 and 1820, while Ancestry also hosts a database version of David Dobson's *Directory of Scots Banished to the American Plantations, 1650–1775*, at **www.ancestry.co.uk/search/collections/48517**.

Ancestry also hosts many additional books by David Dobson concerning Scottish settlers in the USA, in both database and browse formats:

- Scottish Quakers and Early America, 1650–1700
- Scots in New England, 1623–1873
- Scots in the USA and Canada, 1825–1875 (Parts 1–3)
- Directory of Scottish Settlers in North America, 1625–1825 (7 volumes)
- Scots in the Mid-Atlantic Colonies, 1635–1783
- Scots in the Mid-Atlantic States, 1783–1883
- Scottish Soldiers in Colonial America (Parts I–III)
- The Scottish Surnames of Colonial America
- Scots-Dutch Links in Europe and America, 1575–1825
- Scottish-American Wills, 1650–1900
- Scots in the American West, 1783–1883
- Scottish-American Court Records, 1733–1783
- Scottish-American Gravestones, 1700–1900
- Scottish-American Heirs, 1683–1883
- Later Scots-Irish Links, 1575–1725 (Parts 1–4)
- Later Scots-Irish Links, 1725–1825
- Ships from Scotland to America, 1628–1828 (Vol. I & III)
- American Data from the Records of the High Court of the Admiralty of Scotland, 1675–1800,Court, Land, Wills & Financial
- The French and Indian War from Scottish Sources
- The Original Scots Colonists of Early America, 1612–1783
- The Original Scots Colonists of Early America. Supplement 1607–1707

- Scots On the Chesapeake, 1607–1830
- Directory of Scots in the Carolinas, 1680–1830

Ancestry and FindmyPast are both heavily geared towards US-based research, with hundreds of additional databases available, while FamilySearch has many additional datasets freely available. Resources include immigration records and passenger lists, naturalisation records and decennial federal censuses from 1790–1940, as well as many state censuses in the intervening years.

A general gateway site for United States resources is the US GenWeb site at **https://www.usgenweb.org**. The Library of Congress Online Catalog at **https://catalog.loc.gov** can help to source many American publications, photos and media of interest, while the National Archives site at **www.archives.gov** has a great deal of guides and resources on its site for genealogical research. For a list of state archives, visit **www. archives.gov/research/alic/reference/state-archives.html**, while a guide to state historical societies is found at **https://en.wikipedia.org/wiki/ List_of_U.S._state_historical_societies_and_museums**.

From 1892 to 1954, the federal immigration centre at Ellis Island was the main port of entry for immigrants, and digitised passenger lists for all vessels which docked there can be viewed at **www. libertyellisfoundation.org**. Prior to 1892, many who came to the States passed through Castle Garden, the nation's first official immigration centre. From 1820–1892 some 11 million immigrants went through its doors, and their details can be found at **www.familysearch.org/search/**

*The US GenWeb Project platform.*

**collection/1849782**. The United States Citizenship and Immigration Services also has a Genealogy section on its site at **www.uscis.gov**.

Many historic American newspapers have been digitised and made available online, with both Google News and MyHeritage containing substantial collections. Current and historical maps from the US Geological Survey from 1884–2009 are available at **www.usgs.gov**. For access to free census transcripts visit **www.us-census.org**.

The NLS page on Scots in North America (**www.nls.uk/catalogues/ online/scots-abroad/sna**) contains a bibliography of published accounts of visits to the USA and Canada by Scots, ranging from the late seventeenth to the late twentieth century, while its Emigrants Guides to North America database (**www.nls.uk/catalogues/online/scots-abroad/ egna**) may also be of interest.

## Canada

Canada has a particularly strong connection to Scotland, where Scots form the third largest ethnic group after centuries of emigration. From 1670 the Hudson's Bay Company, which traded in furs, was a heavy employer of Scots (particularly those from Orkney), and was later rivalled from 1783 by the Scots-run North West Company. Many Highlanders also settled in the Maritime provinces in the late eighteenth century, particularly in the aftermath of the Clearances, while many Scottish loyalists migrated from the newly formed US in 1783 following the Revolutionary War. A further migration was caused by the failure of the potato crop in Scotland in 1846, affecting many crofting communities.

For many years Scottish Gaelic was spoken in several provinces, and remains a spoken community language in Cape Breton, Nova Scotia, to this day, with its own Gaelic college at St Ann (**https://gaeliccollege. edu**). The first Canadian prime minister was a Glaswegian, Sir John Alexander MacDonald, from 1867–1873 (and again from 1878–1891). For an overview of Scotland's many Canadian connections visit **https:// en.wikipedia.org/wiki/Scottish_Canadians**.

The Library and Archives Canada site (**www.collectionscanada.gc.ca**) contains many wonderful resources and indexes, such as the censuses, records for the military and migration to the country, and various online guides to help with your Canadian research. The *Canadian Gazette* is also available from 1998–present at **www.collectionscanada.gc.ca/databases/ canada-gazette/index-e.html**. Ancestry also has many migration and naturalisation records, including Canadian Passenger Lists from 1865–1935 and Form 30A Ocean Arrivals immigration forms from 1919–24. FamilySearch has a considerable range of records freely available from

*The Library and Archives Canada website hosts many free-to-access databases, including censuses and passenger records.*

each of the main provinces, including several national censuses, vital records, probate material, deeds indexes and more.

For Ontario, the Upper Canada Genealogy site at **www.upper canadagenealogy.com** includes indexes to many records collections, while the Archives of Manitoba site at **www.gov.mb.ca/chc/archives** has several guides and catalogues, including information on how to access the Hudson's Bay Company Archive. The Newfoundland's Grand Banks project at **http://ngb.chebucto.org** hosts many historic articles, passenger lists, directories, vital records, censuses, parish records and more.

Additional Canadian passenger lists can also be found at the Ships Lists site (**www.theshipslist.com**), which also covers the USA, Australia and South Africa. Finally, many Canadian history resources can be found in both English and French at **www.ourroots.ca**.

## Jamaica and the Caribbean

The earliest Scots to Jamaica were some 1,200 prisoners transported there by Cromwell in 1656, with additional settlements following the failure of the Darien Scheme in 1699. Following the Union with England and Wales, Scots then arrived as settlers as citizens of the British Empire, many of them as slave traders, overseers and plantation owners. The story of how north-east Scotland profited from the slave trade in the Caribbean is available at **www.abdn.ac.uk/slavery/index.htm**, with additional resources explored by the NLS at **www.nls.uk/collections/ topics/slavery**.

The Registrar General of Jamaica's site at **www.rgd.gov.jm** has information on how to apply for vital records, while the Jamaica Archives and Records Department has an online presence at **www.jard.gov.jm**. For the British Library's guide to Caribbean holdings, visit **www.bl.uk/ collection-guides/caribbean-collections**, while the National Library of Jamaica has many digital collections online at **www.nlj.gov.jm**.

FamilySearch hosts Jamaican births and baptisms from 1752–1920, while for the Caribbean in general it has births (1590–1928), marriages (1591–1905 and deaths (1790–1906). Ancestry hosts a database entitled 'The Original Scots Colonists of Early America. Caribbean Supplement 1611–1707', while a separate database, 'Former British Colonial Dependencies, Slave Registers, 1813–1834', lists the names of slaves freed following emancipation, including their owners' names, at **www. ancestry.co.uk/search/collections/1129**.

Further gateway sites for Caribbean resources include the Caribbean Genweb Project at **www.rootsweb.ancestry.com/~caribgw** and the Caribbean Genealogy Research site at **www.candoo.com/genresources**.

## South America

By 1822 there were estimated to be 1,200 Scots in Argentina, with their story detailed at the British Settlers in Argentina and Uruguay website at **www.argbrit.org**. This includes records of baptisms, marriages, deaths and burials from St Andrew's Scots Church in Buenos Aires from 1827–1915, transcripts from the National Archives in Buenos Aires and London, and returns from the Argentinian censuses. A preserved version of The Scots in Argentina 1800–1950 website at **https://bit.ly/ ScotsinArgentina** has transcripts of many other useful vital records, while The Saint Andrew's Society of the River Plate website at **www. sasrp.org** explores the Scottish-Argentine community further.

An overview of the story of the Scots living in Patagonia is at **www. electricscotland.com/history/argentina/patchap1.htm** and **www.lifeand work.org/features/looking-back-patagonia**. For those in Chile, visit **https://en.wikipedia.org/wiki/Scottish_Chilean**.

Ancestry hosts a David Dobson book database entitled 'Scots in Latin America', at **www.ancestry.co.uk/search/collections/49340**.

## Australia

Some of the earliest Scots to settle in Australia were crew and convicts arriving with the First Fleet in 1788, although historically Scots law was more lenient with regards to the use of transportation as a form of punishment. Most Scots arrived as free settlers, with many making prominent contributions to the development of the colonies across the continent. Notable early settlers included three of the first six governors of New South Wales: John Hunter from Leith, Lachlan MacQuarie from the island of Ulva (by Mull), and Thomas MacDougall Brisbane from Largs in Ayrshire. For an overview of Scotland's links to Australia visit **https://en.wikipedia.org/wiki/Scottish_Australians**.

The National Archives of Australia (**www.naa.gov.au**) site has various resources, and a guide to family history at **www.naa.gov.au/explore-collection/search-people/researching-your-family**, while the National Library of Australia site hosts a detailed web guide at **www.nla.gov.au/research-guides/family-history**. The library's impressive Trove facility (**https://trove.nla.gov.au**) is well worth searching, containing millions of digitised records, including its superb Australian Newspapers collection, with free to access and fully searchable titles for the continent from 1803–2015, and various *Government Gazettes* from 1832–2012.

ScotlandsPeople hosts free to search Highland and Island Emigration Society passenger lists detailing the passage of some 5,000 emigrants to Australia between 1852 and 1857, with a guide on the records available at **www.scotlandspeople.gov.uk/guides/highland-and-island-emigration-society-records**. The NLS has a Scots in Australasia database listing published accounts of visits to Australia, New Zealand, New Guinea and Oceania at **www.nls.uk/catalogues/online/scots-abroad/scau**, dating from the eighteenth to the twentieth century, as well as a listing of Emigrants' Guides to Australia and New Zealand at **www.nls.uk/catalogues/online/scots-abroad/egaunz** for the nineteenth and twentieth century.

The Ryerson Index (**www.ryersonindex.org**) has a database of almost two and a half million death notices as extracted from contemporary newspapers. The Sydney-based Society of Australian Genealogists (**www.sag.org.au**) also has various online research guides covering everything from adoptions in New South Wales to Ships and Voyages, while the *Australian Dictionary of National Biography* can be consulted at **http://adb.anu.edu.au**.

If your ancestor was transported, consult the Convict Records of Australia site at **https://convictrecords.com.au**. Many additional convict resources are also available on TheGenealogist, Ancestry and FindmyPast platforms, with FindmyPast in particular also hosting a range of more generic Australian offerings. Adelaide-based Gould Genealogy and History is another major genealogical vendor for Australasia, with a large publishing programme, history and genealogy cruises, and expos across the continent, under its 'Unlock the Past' branding: its offerings can be explored at **www.gould.com.au**.

## New Zealand

An overview of Scotland's connections to New Zealand can be read at **https://en.wikipedia.org/wiki/Scottish_New_Zealanders** and **www.tepapa.govt.nz/discover-collections/read-watch-play/history/scots-new-zealand**. The New Zealand History page at **https://nzhistory.govt.nz/culture/home-away-from-home/the-scots** carries some statistical analysis on which parts of Scotland settlers originally arrived from.

The New Zealand Society of Genealogists site at **www.genealogy.org.nz** contains a First Families Index for members, and many other useful resources which can help you to pursue the earliest migrants to the country. Pearl's Pad (**http://pearlspad.net.nz**) equally has many historical resources for tracing migration.

The New Zealand Government has a Births, Deaths and Marriages Online site at **www.bdmonline.dia.govt.nz** which provides indexes for historical vital events, namely births prior to 100 years ago, marriages prior to eighty and deaths prior to fifty years (or at least for those with a date of birth at least eighty years ago). FamilySearch has probate record images for the country from 1860–1962, as well as immigration passenger lists from 1855–1973. The Archives New Zealand catalogue at **www.archway.archives.govt.nz** lists many additional resources.

The Papers Past website (**https://paperspast.natlib.govt.nz**) carries digitised copies of newspaper titles from the nineteenth and twentieth

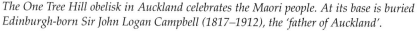

*The One Tree Hill obelisk in Auckland celebrates the Maori people. At its base is buried Edinburgh-born Sir John Logan Campbell (1817–1912), the 'father of Auckland'.*

century, while Victoria University's New Zealand Electronic Text Centre at **http://nzetc.victoria.ac.nz** has many transcribed entries from books and other resources.

For the *Dictionary of New Zealand Biography*, with some 3,000 biographical entries, visit **www.teara.govt.nz/en/biographies**. The Otago Settlers Museum website at **www.toituosm.com** has an online catalogue which permits you to search for holdings, while further resources for Otago and the Southlands can be explored through **www.otago.ac.nz/library** and **http://otago.ourheritage.ac.nz**.

## India

If your Scottish family member made it to India, the first port of call for research is the Families in British India Society site at **www.fibis.org**, which includes listings from cemeteries, directories, military records, photographs, publications, schools, probate indexes, vital and parish records and more.

The British Library's India Office Family History Search index at **http://indiafamily.bl.uk/UI/Home.aspx** lists some 300,000 vital records, while the NLS's India Papers collection at **www.nls.uk/collections/official-publications/india-papers** includes information on family history resources and the Medical History of British India project.

FindmyPast hosts several British India-themed databases, including the following:

- British India Office Births & Baptisms
- British India Office Deaths & Burials
- British India Office Marriages
- British India Office Wills & Probate
- British India Office Army & Navy Pensions
- British India Office Assistant Surgeons

FamilySearch also holds the following databases:

- India Births and Baptisms, 1786–1947
- India Deaths and Burials, 1719–1948
- India Marriages, 1792–1948

The British Association for Cemeteries in South Asia site at **www.bacsa.org.uk** carries an index to cemetery inscriptions in areas previously occupied by the East India Company. Additional burials may be found via the Kabristan Archives at **www.kabristan.org.uk**.

# FURTHER READING

Bigwood, Rosemary (2006) *The Scottish Family Tree Detective*. Manchester: Manchester University Press

Bissett-Smith, G.T. (1907). *Vital Registration: a Manual of the Law and Practice Concerning the Registration of Births, Marriages and Deaths*. Edinburgh: W. Green and Sons.

Brown, Callum G. (1997) *Religion and Society in Scotland since 1707*. Edinburgh: Edinburgh University Press.

Clarke, Tristram (2011) *Tracing Your Scottish Ancestors – The Official Guide (6th ed)* . Edinburgh, Birlinn Ltd.

Hamilton-Edward, Gerald (1986) *In Search of Scottish Ancestry*. Chichester: Phillimore & Co. Ltd.

Holton, Graham (Ed.) (2019) *Tracing Your Ancestors Using DNA*. Barnsley: Pen & Sword Family History.

Innes, Sir Thomas of Learney (1956) *Scots Heraldry*. Edinburgh: Oliver & Boyd.

Kopittke, Rosemary (2012) *ScotlandsPeople: The Place to Launch Your Scottish Research*. Adelaide: Unlock the Past.

Nisbet, Kenneth (2013) *The Register of Corrected Entries and Its Use for Family History*. Edinburgh: Scottish Genealogy Society

Paton, Chris (2014) *Tracing Your Family History on the Internet (Second Edition)* . Barnsley: Pen & Sword Family History.

Paton, Chris (2019) *Tracing Your Irish Family History on the Internet (Second Edition)* . Barnsley: Pen & Sword Family History.

Paton, Chris (2019) *Tracing Your Scottish Ancestry Through Church and State Records*. Barnsley: Pen & Sword Family History.

Paton, David (2006) *The Clergy and the Clearances: The Church and the Highland Crisis 1790–1850*. Edinburgh: John Donald.

Prebble, John (2002) *Culloden*. London: Pimlico.

Prebble, John (1982) *The Highland Clearances*. London: Penguin Books.

Roulston, William J. (2018) *Researching Ulster Ancestors: The Essential Genealogical Guide to Early Modern Ulster, 1600–1800*. Belfast, Ulster Historical Foundation.

Simpson, Grant (2009) *Scottish Handwriting 1150–1650: An Introduction to the Reading of Documents*. Edinburgh: John Donald Short Run Press.

Sinclair, Cecil (2000). *Jock Tamson's Bairns: A History of the Records of the General Register Office for Scotland*. Edinburgh: General Register Office for Scotland.

Smout, T.C. (1997) *A Century of the Scottish People 1830–1950*. London: Fontana Press

Smout, T.C. (1998) *A History of the Scottish People 1560–1830*. London: Fontana Press

Steel, D.J. (1970) *National Index of Parish Registers Volume XII: Sources for Scottish Genealogy and Family History*. Chichester: Phillimore and Co. Ltd.

Watts, Christopher T. and Michael J. (2002). *My Ancestor Was a Merchant Seaman*. London: Society of Genealogists.

# INDEX